"BOY NO NAME"

The Charles Lee Story

written by: *Charles Lee*

General Information

"Boy with NO NAME"

The Charles Lee Story

Charles Lee

Copyright © 2019: **Charles Lee**

Cover Design: TP Graphics- *Shantorya Kelley*

Self-Published by Charles Lee

Editor: *Terry L. Ware Sr.*

ISBN: *9781709481598*

1. *Nonfiction 2. Autobiography 3. Motivation 5. Inspiration*

First Edition

Dedication

I dedicate this book to my Beautiful wife, & my Awesome 3 kids.

To my mother and father that never gave up, no matter how hard their fight became!

My two sisters that showed me what real women Gladiators are.

My two older brothers, & brother-in-law, they never let me forget about my Chicago heritage.

Every incredible hard worker at **That's My Dog**, any location.

The Awesome Staff & every Volunteer of **That's My Child**.

To 862 Students that have been mentored through **That's My Child Youth Organization**.

To every broken student that feels alone.

Last but not least, to the doctor that told my mother, I wouldn't make it!

God definitely had a purpose for my life, and I endeavor to continue to allow Him to lead me so that purpose will continue to *FLOURISH*!

Foreword

WoW! The "Boy with NO NAME" is an outstanding read! From beginning to end you will be in tune and your mind on edge while reading through each chapter. Charles Lee, "The Boy With No Name", has been on an up and down journey of life, all of which has made him into the great man he is today.

With this book, I encourage you to feel the words as you read them, allow them to penetrate your mind as you read through this story of his life. His journey will show you just how great God is. Just when we think that we have it all figured out, He will take us beyond what we thought we could do.

There are times when God needs you to hear from Him that He will allow you to get in certain situations where you have nowhere to turn but to Him. You see that within Charles journey, he could have chosen to give up, blame God for his actions, but he choose to listen and hear God out. Though he may not have fully understood at times, he kept listening and was determined to follow His instructions. That's how God wants us to endeavor to be, to lean and depend on Him and not our own understanding.

The Boy With No Name has become a great man in his community, in his church, and in his family. Isn't it something how God will take a child with no name and make him into a man that many will desire to know! "I will make you into a great nation. I will bless you and make you famous, and you will be a blessing to others"- Genesis 12:2. God has certainly taken the "Boy with NO NAME" and made his name great. There's so much more greatness ahead so be sure to keep your ears open for the name, Charles Lee…

Author Terry L. Ware Sr.
CEO B.O.S.S. Publishing, LLC

Table of Contents

Dedication.................................*iv*

Foreword................................*vi*

Introduction..............................*2*

Chapter 1

   Prison.................................*12*

Chapter 2

   The Boy With No Name.....................*16*

Chapter 3

   5-6 Years Old............................*19*

Chapter 4

   ICKIES................................*25*

Chapter 5

   54ᵀᴴ and Aberdeen- 8 Years Old..............*35*

Chapter 6

43rd & Calumet (Hustle Block)...................40

Chapter 7

JR. Getting Murdered............................48

Chapter 8

Getting Shot...................................52

Chapter 9

The Move to Montgomery......................58

Chapter 10

Alternative School............................. 63

Chapter 11

The Crew.....................................68

Chapter 12

Dating Older Women..........................72

Chapter 13

My Father Returns............................79

Chapter 14

Job Corps....................................84

Chapter 15

Love of my Life...............................95

Chapter 16

Moved to Florida............................98

Chapter 17

Headed to Jail...............................105

Chapter 18

My Jail Experience........................118

Chapter 19

Moving Back to Montgomery............125

Chapter 20

Laurali.......................................129

Chapter 21

Starting a Mentoring Program............135

Chapter 22

That's My Dog..............................143

Chapter 23

Charles Lee JR.............................154

Chapter 24

That's My Child………......………....………160

Chapter 25

What the Devil Meant for Evil...…………...……169

Chapter 26

That's My Dog JR.………………....……….…..175

Testimonials..................................…......*181*

"Boy with NO NAME"

The Charles Lee Story

written by: *Charles Lee*

Table Talk | Against the Odds

"That's my dog!" This is the unforgettable phrase that you might hear from one of River Region's finest, Charles Lee. This Montgomerian is trailblazing through the capital city to give back to and support community teens that are less fortunate and facing hardships of violence and poverty. Charles's three word catchphrase has morphed into establishing a safe haven and a plethora of opportunities for adolescents to stay off the streets. His zest for helping youth reach their all-time potential is contagious, and he is relentlessly spreading his passion throughout the community. Charles's spectacular efforts led him to be chosen as the 2017

recipient of the *Alabama Young Professional's Hero award* and the *2017 Leadership Montgomery Unit award.*

RSVP Montgomery was delighted to interview this local business owner and community activist as he shared his candid personal life story, a story which ultimately inspired him to guide and nurture the lives of our youth. Through his transparency, it was evident that this charismatic civic leader is making an impactful difference in the young lives of our future generation through innovative ways to matriculate teens into mainstream society. Not only did his inspiring efforts move us, we

were intrigued to hear his story unfold, and how *he* transformed his life through unwavering determination.

At the tender age of 13, Charles lost *all* hope that he would live and make a positive contribution to society. Growing up in one of America's most dangerous cities, he lived in a gang-riddled neighborhood in Chicago that did not afford him with many opportunities. Charles says, "I was born prematurely, a crack baby weighing 2lbs and 7oz, I spent the first two years of my life in the hospital battling with bronchitis and hepatitis C. I wasn't expected to live past the age of

By Kimberley Carter Spivey | Photos by Brooke Glassford / Colorbox Photographers

Introduction

Thank you for taking the time to read this book. I pray this book inspires you and you will take it to someone and inspire them!

The "Boy with NO NAME" is the ultimate story of HOPE! I wanted to share my testimony with everyone, to show the world how God can take any underdog, dip him in his blood, and turn him into a champion.

This is a story about a young man from the southside of Chicago, Illinois with two parents that had an addiction to crack cocaine. On July 29, 1982, at 2:45 _____ was born. Considered a "crack baby", very premature, weighing 2 pounds and 3 ounces, with his lungs collapsing, and many other illnesses, the doctor told his mother he wouldn't survive a week. Looking at his Condition it was very easy for every doctor and nurse to count him out. 90% of premature babies in that condition never make it out of the hospital breathing.

As his mother experienced surgery after surgery, watching his health decline, she started to believe the doctors and lose faith. So his mother decided to decline and not add a name to his Birth certificate. Shockingly, to everyone's surprise, this "Boy With No Name", survived not only his first week but he was approaching 2 years old, healthy enough to go home for the first time where his two older sisters awaited him.

Although his health was getting better every day, his parent's addiction got worse. Without proper parental guidance, they were forced to raise themselves. He joined a gang and started selling drugs at the age of 11, and both of his sisters became pregnant within five months of each other at the age of 13 & 14 years old. By the age of 13, he was shot in the chest and got arrested for the first time at age 16.

He moved to Florida at the age of 18 years old, started dealing drugs there and ended up in jail. While he was serving his time, he was introduced to a Savior named Jesus Christ. He then asked that savior why was his childhood so jacked up? The Savior told him, "because I have a purpose for your life, I need you to go back and redirect as many youths as you can." That's exactly what he did! He went from coaching local sports basketball, football, and baseball to starting a Youth Organization called That's My Child. He mentored intercity youth, working to keep them from choosing the same path he chose. In the process, he also started a very successful business called, That's My Dog.

After he realized most of his student's problems pinpointed from generation poverty, he made it his mission to break that cycle by starting the first-ever all Teenage Managed and Operated Restaurant called, That's My Dog Jr. Employing & training students from the community with Workforce Development, & Entrepreneurship while making sure they would have every tool they would need to become financially independent without having to turn to selling drugs or robbing others.

He has become a household name and now, The "Boy with NO NAME", name, is being printed in Newspapers and Magazines nationally for the work he is doing in his community!

Ladies & Gentleman his Name is:

CHARLES LEE!

Mohona Lee

The Wife of Charles Lee

Words cannot express how proud of you I am for how far you have come. You have prospered and grown so much since we started this long journey. I am so honored to be your wife! You have done so much in this community and have changed so many kid's lives. I knew you'd always make it this far. You are a go-getter and deserve every ounce of respect you get from this community.

This journey started when we were young, our 1st place together we slept on our bags of clothes that 1st night and a few more nights after that. You promised you were going to take care of me and you have. When we found out you were going to be incarcerated, you made sure I was not going to do without while you were gone. On one occasion that I visited, you told me God gave you the vision to help the youth, you also told me all the ideas God gave you.

I was so happy to see how excited you were, all I could think was how much I love you.

The day we decided to get Laurali, you did not think twice about it, "she is our family", you said. So many court dates later and visitations and after all the dedication, the first blessing, an angel sent straight from heaven, Laurali finally came home with us. This was the new chapter of the best days of our lives.

We came up with this idea to make a hotdog stand because no one in the city of Montgomery had this brilliant idea. We did not know it would be the beginning of change and joy in the city of Montgomery. "Hey, Laurali what do you think of the name That's My Dog?" "Dad I like that name". Then, came the infamous That's My Dog! Soon after, your dream came true to help the youth, you came up with That's My Child.

We prayed and fasted for the blessing of another child. 16 years later, some people may have given up on God but you did not. Then, God did it, a handsome baby boy was born on October of 2016, Charles Lee Jr, aka CJ. We found out at a young age that he had Autism, but you never let that get to you. God knows what he is doing he blessed us with an amazing son.

You wanted more kids but you said, "When God wants us to have more, He will let us know", and He did just that. Elijah Gabriel Lee, was born in June of 2019. You were so happy to have another child but to find out it was another boy; you could not believe God was blessing you so much.

You amaze me so much; most men who have been through what you have been through would not try so hard to give us a great life. I am grateful for the amazing man you are today. It has not always been easy but you did not give up on us and I will not give up on you. I do not want to do this thing called life with anyone else. We have been through so much together and we have learned the good, bad, and ugly about each other and I would not change a thing. I thank god for you every single day! I Love You!

Laurali Tolleson

The Daughter of Charles Lee

I hope everyone loves my dad's book, "Boy with NO NAME", the way I do. I am so proud of my dad; he has a great voice throughout this community. I pray my dad can have more impact on this community as opportunities come his way. My dad is a great thinker and loves to be the best possible person he can be and he only wants the best for me, our family, and everyone around him. He has always had a robust character and is a great leader.

My dad has done so much for me through my rough childhood. Even when we didn't have much money, he always found a way to provide and still get us phones and electronics or whatever we would need and want, that's the kind of person he is. He has always done the best he possibly could to make us happy.

Throughout my life, I haven't always been the nicest to my dad because of my confusion. My dad never deserved the way I used to treat him when I was little. I was always embarrassed because we looked different. Now that I am older, I realized that was so silly, and ridiculous. I know now that you should never treat someone rudely even if you are confused because they look different, especially someone that stepped up and became your father when no one else would.

My dad took me in and made me his daughter. He paid for the lawyers when he didn't even know me! He signed the custody papers and made me have a better life. I didn't have to sit in foster care any longer because he cared. Even though he may not be my biological father, he is still 10000 times better than anyone else ever could be.

He was the one who made it to the court dates and acted like he wanted to be in my life even though he barely knew me as a little girl. Even if all of a sudden my biological dad showed up, he would never get as much respect or get called anything close to the word FATHER. I have a father that deserves way more respect than any biological father. I'm grateful for how my dad serves his community, and I'm thankful to call him MY DAD, Charles Lee.

Chapter 1

Prison

What an awesome day on the beach. The smell of fresh seafood cooking everywhere, live reggae playing in the background from Bamboo Willie's, bushwhackers floating with an extra shot of 151 Bacardi on top. Everyone bought out the boats today. The girls in skimpy bikinis everywhere. The weather was just right. Sunny but the breeze from the ocean was breathless. I've just made $5,000 in 2 hours selling some of the best cocaine Pensacola beach has ever seen.

And for myself, I've just rolled up some of the best marijuana I have ever smoked. We're all partying on my friend's yacht that he just bought last week. Drinking and listening to Biggie Smalls "It Was All a Dream." And right before I could take my first pull, I hear the slamming of steel doors, WHAM!!! "Inmates, on your feet!" And I realize, this is truly all a dream.

Reality set in every roll call as my feet hit the floor, that I was still incarcerated. 149 prisons are being operated by the Florida DOC, housing 101,424 men and women who can do nothing but daydream and try to reconcile their past. For now, one of those men rusting in Escambia Prison was me! Thinking to myself, "What have I gotten myself into? Who is writing this life for me? Is it the pen or the paper that is causing my life destruction?" Hey God, are you there? Can you explain why my childhood was so dark, lonely and filled with tragic moments?

Shortly after my questions, He came into my life. Then my dreams at night started to shift. I went from dreaming the life I used to lead as a free man on the beach, going to the best parties with the best drugs, up until my incarceration. Into having dreams of how I can change a culture of kids who feel dark, lonely, and whom lives are filled with tragic moments before they end up incarcerated, like me. I started having dreams where I was in a huge building where kids were coming in and out, and their hearts were being converted – not only to have a love for themselves but love for their community. It was called The S.P.O.T.

The more my relationship grew with Christ, the more I would have those dreams. The more I saw the dreams, the more I believed they could come true. But where would I start this program? Downtown Pensacola? Scenic Boulevard? Fairfield? He said, "No, I need you to go back to Montgomery, Alabama." And I said, "The Devil is a liar!" I had vowed never to return to Montgomery, Alabama.

The next morning, I used my first phone call to call my wife. She told me about a dream that she had where we moved back to Montgomery, Alabama.

Chapter 2

First Miracle:

Boy with NO

NAME

July 29, 1982

On the South Side of Chicago, in the Englewood Hospital, my mother was being rushed into an emergency C-section because I had stopped breathing. As I was cut from my mother's womb, I headed straight to the operating table where I fought the first fight for my life. Due to my mother's intake of drugs from her addiction, I had a terrible case of bronchitis and Hepatitis C. The doctors told my mother that I may not make it through the week. Therefore, she never added a name to my birth certificate, she felt it may be a little useless.

And then the fight truly began. The doctors and nurses referred to me as "The Boy With No Name." I spent my first 2 years in the ICU fighting to live. During these two years, I stopped breathing a total of 49 times, and flatlined 3 times and had to be brought back to life. I wasn't expected to see my 5th birthday. The doctors didn't know the plan God had for my life. Even after I left the hospital, I wasn't expected to make it to five years old. I was welcomed home to my two sisters, Latasha and Angela Lee.

Chapter 3

5-6 years old

So when I finally made it to the age the doctors said I wouldn't see, I could remember being in a neighborhood called Englewood, on 62nd Place, in a ran down two-story duplex where the back stairs gave me nightmares. Our landlord lived up top on the second floor, her name was Miss Louise. The neighborhood was infested with crack and filled with gang violence, but it was so fun. One thing I came to learn about Chicago was that every neighborhood was run by a different gang, whether it was BDs (Black Disciples), GDs (Gangster Disciples), Vice Lords, or Black Stones, the list goes on and on. This particular neighborhood was run by the Gangster Disciples.

A lot of my dad's side of the family and his childhood friends lived on this street. I was always told stories of how before my dad was addicted to crack, he was a big-time board member of the Black Disciples, my father was a legend to his friends. I had never seen that side of him, because growing up I only saw the addiction. One of his childhood friends gave me the nickname I still have today, Bippy. Everyone in the family called me Bippy; I swear half of the family didn't even know my real name. How I ended up with the nickname was that one night everyone was making up names for me because I still had no name on my birth certificate, and my dad's friend came up with Bippy.

Miss Louise had a granddaughter named Leelee, and we were the same age. She wasn't the prettiest girl in the world, but to me she was beautiful. I used to sneak Leelee Nutty-Buddies and milk when no one was paying attention. We went to kindergarten and first grade together. We walked to school together, and I protected her in and out of school. She gave me my first kiss. Neither one of us knew what we were doing, which was probably because we were only five. Leelee's mother was killed at a very young age, and we used to talk about that a lot. She would cry, and I would tell her that she was lucky because she had a guardian angel watching over her every day.

We knew everybody on the block. Two houses down from us was Ms. Angeline, my father's grandmother, who lived to be 104 years old. I was scared to go visit her because she did voodoo; we were always scared to visit her because we didn't want to end up being dolls.

Next door to Ms. Angeline was my aunt Fannie B's building. Fannie B was probably about 98 pounds soaking wet, but she didn't mess around. She would cuss you out in a heartbeat, but make it sound so funny. Every time I would knock on her door, she would say, "Who knock?" And I would say, "It's me, Bippy!" She would say, "Bippy, that's your little fat ass?" She would have card parties every Friday night.

Fannie B would give me cigarettes at a party and tell me to throw them in the toilet. I'd take a puff on the way to the bathroom like I was the man. I can still remember my first time taking a puff, I couldn't stop coughing. Her and my mother were very close; both were super gangster. Not only would my mother cuss you out, but she would also beat you up, weighing in at 390 pounds soaking wet. I once saw her arguing with Miss Louise on the second floor. She opened up the window and threw her out. I thought she was dead. It was at that point when I realized why no one messed with my mother.

Right before my 6th birthday, I remember going to bed and my dad and his friends were in the house partying, drinking, and getting high. But I really couldn't sleep, so around midnight, I went out for something to drink. I didn't see my dad or any of his friends. But the back door was cracked, so I decided to walk outside to see if they were out there. When I opened up the door I saw my dad and his friends all laying on the porch. I started screaming, "Somebody, please, help! Help! My dad and his friends are dead!" Finally, one of my neighbors walked over and said, "Bippy, relax, they're not dead, they're just high." Then, I pulled the needle out of my dad's arm and the plastic bands that were tied around his arm. I cleaned his arm up by wiping off the blood and pulled him up close to me and sat with him until he woke up about three hours later.

One night, I heard someone pounding on the door, it was my grandmother, my dad's mom, and my uncle Donnie, Aunty Roseanne. Everyone was crying hysterically. My father and mother asked, "What's going on?" And everyone yelled, "It's Fannie, it's Fannie!" They began to tell the story.

My grandmother and my uncle were headed home to Park Ridge, Illinois when my Uncle Donnie had a hunch to go check on Fannie B. When they got to her door, they knocked a couple of times, and then my uncle Donnie kicked down the door. And there, they found Fannie B in the bathtub soaking in her blood. She had been stabbed 72 times. That was the first funeral that I attended.

Her killer was never revealed or brought to justice, but the family had a hunch of who did it. Grandma never discussed it after that. RIP Fannie B. Fannie B's death messed everyone up. That was the first time I ever saw my father stick a needle in his arm.

Chapter 4

Ickies

Shortly after Fannie B's death, we moved on 23rd and State Street. State Street ran from downtown Chicago all the way close to Michigan with nothing but projects along the way. We just moved into one of them called, The Ickies. My first thought of these projects was "Wow, they're huge!" The Ickies was a building of 16 floors with 22 apartments per floor. Luckily, we stayed on the second floor, apartment 202, because the elevators rarely worked.

I thought Englewood was tough, but the Ickies were ten times rougher. At least in Englewood, you could go to your apartment individually, but here, it was like we all lived together in one huge apartment. If you had a problem with someone, you were guaranteed to see them in that building before the day was out.

Within a couple of weeks, my father had found a new "Get high buddy," Andre. He was married to a lady named Christine. They had 3 kids also, that was exactly mismatched of us. Two older boys and one younger daughter. We became like the Brady Bunch.

We all became close and as the relationship between Andre and my father got closer, the relationship between my mother and Christine became closer, and we the kids followed. We all attended Dr. Hale Williams Elementary. Christine was the only parent at the time that wasn't an addict. So while my father, my mama, and Andre were smoking together in our 2nd-floor apartment, we would all have to go to Christine place on the 5th floor. When we came home, my mom would tell all of her friends, "Oh! It's time to go." But some of them didn't want to leave because they knew there was still dope remaining, so my mom would get physical and beat them out.

In Englewood, my parents were functioning addicts. They were still working and doing their best to take care of us, but when we moved to the Ickies, things changed. My sister Latasha became the parent. She'd walk us to and from wherever we needed to go. We'd go to the store together, she'd walk us to school, she was our protector. The day after we moved in, my sister and I were walking to the store and these dudes approached me like they wanted to fight. My sister Latasha burst into a windmill motion, rotating her arms like a tornado. I don't know if those guys were scared or confused, but they sure did leave us alone.

I had my first experience with gang violence in the Ickies. My father was smoking crack like it was his job. Conveniently for him, the biggest drug dealer on our block, Luccane, lived on the 16th floor. At all hours of the night, you'd hear people looking for a fix yelling "Luccane", from the ground floor. My father built up debt with Luccane. One day, I was walking with my father down the street and 16 men jumped out and began to whoop my father like nothing my six-year-old self, had ever seen before. Everyone was swinging blind, and my father ended up sneaking out of the pile. Luccane and his homeboys were still jumping somebody.

My First Church Experience

Christine loved the church. She'd have us going to different churches all week. Christine gave me my first true church experience. She'd pay us if we learned scriptures or all the books of the Bible. After church, she'd take us out for hamburgers and ice cream. When we were hungry, she'd share her food stamps with us as well.

Eventually, we settled in at a church named Mount Calvary, which had been one of the church's Christine took us to. It was a long ride away because it was on the West Side. At first, the people there would scare me because they would get out of their seat, and start hollering, shouting, dancing, and running. I asked, "Why are these people acting so wild?" Christine said, "They have the Holy Ghost." I'm like, if these people have ghosts in them, I got to get out of here, (LoL). We eventually fell in love with Mount Calvary church. I and my sisters joined the youth choir, called the Sunshine band. My sister Angela would be hooting and hollering in the pews at eight years old. We could see she was receiving that ghost they had spoken of, "Holy Ghost." During altar call one Sunday, Angela told Tasha and me to go up to the front with her and ask the Pastor if he could pray for our parents to stop smoking crack. Confused and nervous, we walked up to the pulpit. The preacher leaned down to us and asked, "What do you want to pray for?" Angela said confidently, "For my momma and daddy to stop smoking crack."

Two weeks later, Mount Calvary was having their revival. Christine had convinced my mother and father to come to church as they were in the middle of getting high. I don't know if it was the drugs, but they agreed. They came to Mount Calvary with drugs in their pockets. The Pastor called them to the altar and had my mother to empty her pockets and my father followed, putting their crack right there on the altar in front of everyone.

After that day, my parents were committed to change. Both of them stopped smoking and ended up getting jobs with the Board of Education as custodial workers. Even though we were committed to change, that didn't mean our neighborhood was ready to make the same commitment.

One day as we came home from church, right as we were getting out of the car we could hear some shots. We waited a few minutes then headed upstairs to our apartment. The shots we heard was a man getting murdered right in front of our door. He was shot multiple times at close range in the head and all of his blood, guts, and brains was gushing into our apartment. Then our neighbor came out to say, "Son one day that will be you." I told her; "The devil is a liar, get behind me Satan!"

My Big Brothers

I saw two older guys who kind of looked like me (but super light-skinned) coming up to our apartment. I asked my mother and father, "Who are these guys? Are they coming to move our furniture?" It was then explained to me that they were my two older brothers, both 7-8 years older than me, that I'd never met before from another relationship. Their mother was going through some stuff and had put them out, so my dad brought them in. My mother couldn't understand how their mother could put them out, she was always angry that they were now her responsibility. I felt proud of having big brothers now, but Charles and Shaun weren't feeling me. "Faggot, punk, sissy," they'd call me. All I wanted was for them to embrace me. Other than that, life was good.

Now that my parents weren't smoking anymore, life was different. My father and mother were working more, they had more money, and they dressed differently. We were a better family, but that didn't mean my parents weren't being tested.

One night, my dad and I went to the store. A guy whom my father owed money (a big-time drug dealer from Englewood) pulled a gun out on him and said, "Pay me my money right now." My father looked him dead in his eyes and said, "You can shoot me, my life belongs to God." Twenty seconds later, my cousins rolled up with their guns and chased the man away. On the way home, I couldn't stop feeling like my dad was a real-life hero. He stared the barrel of a gun in the face! I couldn't wait to get home and tell everyone how gangster my father was! The love he had for God could've gotten him killed, and he didn't care.

This was a brand-new world for us, trying to live life through the church. My dad became a Deacon at Mount Calvary. Mom and Dad were in the choir there, and my siblings and I were in the Sunshine Band, the kids' choir. Since my dad's siblings were still getting high, all of our relatives saw him as the success of the family. He was such a role model in the community that he convinced his mother, his sister Patricia Bates, and other family members to come to church. They'd seen his life change and they wanted to be a part of it.

Although some from the neighborhood weren't convinced that my dad was a changed man, they would test him all the time. I remember one man named Junior came up and asked my dad "Are you sure you're saved?" Then slapped him real hard and said, "Now you have to turn the other cheek." We thought Dad was about to beat him down, but instead, dad turned the other cheek. We ended up moving out of the Ickies, onto bigger and better things.

Chapter 5

54th and Aberdeen –

8 years old

I was 8 years old now and in the 3rd grade. I was going to Holmes Elementary; we had moved in with Christine and Andre on 54th and Aberdeen, and we were going to church all the time. All of us lived in a duplex together; you could still call it the hood, but it wasn't anything like the Ickies.

Now that our parents were living the "saved" life, our lives were on lockdown, rules controlled every move we made:

1.Don't go outside. Drugs are outside.

2.Don't listen to rap. Rappers talk about drugs.

To pass the time, my siblings and I began to write and perform our own plays, we made up dances, and tried our very best to copy the personalities we saw on In Living Color and Martin. My older brother and I would sometimes put on dresses and pretended to be WANDA and SHANAYNA. One time the neighbor came and knocked on the door while we were going over a skit and my brother and I still had on dresses. He was like what in the world is going on. Such a fun day that we all still laugh about until this day; we were just trying to bond since we were confined to the house. We got to grow closer as siblings because we never got to leave. Eventually, we got bored, and the rules started to be broken. The front door was begging to be opened, so we snuck outside. Daddy's muffler was so loud that you could hear him coming, so we just bet on getting back inside before we got caught.

Our parents always said we couldn't go outside, they hadn't made any rules about other people coming in, so we started having house parties. We let the whole block into the house. Whenever we heard that muffler getting closer, we'd rush people out the back door. One time, my siblings threw a huge party while my parents were at church. Just like usual, we heard the muffler coming and shooed everyone out through the back door. We thought everything was straight. However, when my parents opened the back door, there everybody was in the back foyer, chilling as though nothing was wrong. We were sure we were dead.

Instead, our parents took us out for pizza that night, it was so strange. The next Sunday, we went to a brand-new church. The Pastors name was Reverend D. Hinton and his sermon was on sparing the rod and spoiling the child, which I found out meant beating the hell out of your kids. All of us had mostly forgotten about our party, but my father put a new latch on our back door. When we got home from church, we were told to look at a picture, bend over the kitchen table, and one by one, we were hit with a 2x4. Latasha went first, but she was everyone's favorite so she just got two little taps. Angela was nobody's favorite child back then. They ended up breaking the 2x4 over her head. Not a problem for them, they just got another one and we all got whooped. Yup, my parents were "saved!"

We were back at Mount Calvary the next week. We went to church 3 days out of the week. Tuesday was a rehearsal for the Sunshine Band, Wednesday was bible study, and we went to Sunday morning and evening service since daddy was one of the head Deacons. My father was extremely popular in all of his church roles: he was a Deacon, Choir member, and Mr. Fix-It. That meant he was in church at least 6 days out of the week. And then the phone calls began. Women would call our house asking for "prayers" at 2 am. The phone calls went from "prayer" to "Can you fix this? Can you help with my son?" To allegations of my father sleeping with those same women.

My father had two friends. One named Deacon Melton and Deacon Edward. All of that came to a head, and one day, my father called us in the room and let us know he was moving out, he and my mom were separating. It was no surprise because the church was already talking about it. Shortly after, more allegations came against Deacon Milton and Deacon Edward, and even the Pastor cheating on his wife. I remember feeling bad for my mother because of the cheating, and she felt ashamed to return to the church with the same women. Just like that, we were back at square one.

Chapter 6

43ʳᵈ & Calumet

(Hustle Block)

By the time I turned 11, my father was just gone. We didn't know where he was. When he lost his crib, he was just MIA. My momma thought it would be a good thing for me to go to Rosetta's where my cousin Mane could teach me how to be a man. I ended up going over there and my sisters came over to visit. At Rosetta's, it was like every man for themselves.

Everybody's kids were there. But it wasn't the typical house where someone was cooking dinner by 6 pm. If you wanted to eat you had to learn how to survive. One day I went to talk to Mane, I told Mane, "Hey cuzz me and my sisters are pretty hungry and need some food!" He took me to 43rd and Calumet and gave me ten dime bags of crack cocaine and said: "Here go your food." I said, "How am I gonna eat this?" He said, "With this hustle, you will never go hungry again for the rest of your life."

Every $10 bag I sold, I got $2. Mane had a way with his dope; he would put a little detergent in it while he cooked it up, the junkies loved it. Before I could start officially selling dope, Mane told me I had to join a gang, Gangster Disciples (GDs). I joined with my cousin Rob, and three other guys named JR., Pudgy, and little Piggy. I was 11, Rob was 12, JR. was 12 Piggy was 12, and Pudgy was 13. We all joined at the same time during a session meeting and we didn't have to get jumped in. At the session, they let us know the expectations. We did, however, have to complete an Initiation.

We had to Rob this older gentleman named Mr. Smith one Friday night after he cashed his check, he was about 70 years old. They were so excited about doing this, the whole time I felt it was not right. So Friday was here, and we saw him walking down the block as usual and we all bomb rushed him, taking his wallet and cash. They even started beating him up pretty bad. I had to remind them that the mission was not to kill him, but only bring back the money. I felt so bad for Mr. Smith looking back at him laying on that sidewalk as we ran away. It made us official and we were now Gangster Disciples.

We had to go to weekly meetings, and once a month we had to attend a regional meeting. We had to pay dues every week, $2 a meeting. We had to learn literature about the gang: what the six points of the star represented, we had to learn the creed, everything.

The younger people were the most valuable in the organization; the older people had so many strikes with the police that they were likely to go to jail for a long time if they got picked up. They knew if a kid got picked up, we'd get let out the next day.

A mouth shot is what you get if you make a small mistake. You get dapped up and then punched in the mouth. Bonecrusher, a 6'7 man, was the designated mouth shotter. If you didn't know your creed, Bonecrusher would dap you up one time. A violation is when you get beat up by 2 or 3 huge men. You don't want to get a violation. By the end of my time in the GDs, I got one mouth shot and one violation from Mane because my uncle stole all my drugs.

I learned all my literature. I represented 16 GDs because I knew everything (mostly because I didn't want to get mouth shots.) My homeboy Piggy couldn't even read, but they let him in because his family was so plugged into the neighborhood. The GDs started an area coordinator position for the 16 and under, and they asked me to be the area coordinator to make sure everyone was on point with their literature. Piggy was my assistant. On the block, everyone that sold drugs had to pick one hour to do security. If you were security, you had to yell the codeword if you saw police. If you didn't say it, you got a violation. We had pit bulls trained to bark when we saw police on the roof.

That's when I started selling drugs. Mane gave me ten rocks the first time, then twenty more – I was the most grinding' person out there. I would be on the block until the police made me go home. In Chicago, we had a curfew, so if you were underage the police would pick you up and take you home. I couldn't tell you how many times I'd keep the rocks in my mouth wrapped in plastic. Before I went on the block, I had to learn how to swallow an 8 ball and retrieve it from my poop. At 2 o'clock in the morning, I'd be asking Mane for more rocks.

My cousin Rob wasn't a hustler; he was always messing with the girls and had his first child around 13 or 14, he'd bring the rocks back and say, "wasn't nobody out there today." For me, I was hitting that block, I was just out there hustling. My cousin would take us with him to go buy the drugs, and then he'd show us how to cook the drugs. Sometimes, I'd end up cooking all the drugs for him. The first time I cooked, I messed up the drugs by adding too much baking soda, but I learned quick.

One day, I had 30 rocks on me and my uncle rolled up behind me. He was a big-time thief that loved to get high as well, and he knew I had the drugs on me. We talked for 30 minutes and when we were done, the rocks were gone. I had to go tell Mane I lost all the drugs. I got a violation behind that.

I decided that day after getting beat up, I wanted to sell drugs for myself. I had already learned how to cook it properly; all I needed to do was save $180 to buy my own 8ball to get started. I reached out to Mane supplier and I bought my own drugs and started selling for myself. He was mad about me selling, but he couldn't stop me. I was 11, I wasn't just only thinking about getting money; I didn't want to get beat up again.

We were different kinds of dealers. Mane had been making bad batches and charging a lot for them. When it was my drugs, I would take whatever money I could. People would fight, but I was always cool, making people laugh. People would try to barter with me using toys, video games, even offering to suck my penis. People would rent me their cars; I learned how to drive at age 11. That was all the fun of being on the block. But there were bad times, too. Chicago police were the worst, they would ravage through your belongings. They'd come on the block and choke you out, then take all of your money, beat you up, and you'd never go to jail. They'd even throw coffee in your face, it was a jungle, and that was their way of handling it. Blondie was a white woman police officer known all over the South Side. She would fight like a dude. And the worst part was, the murders.

Chapter 7

JR. Getting

Murdered

Me and JR. started getting really close but he wasn't much of a drug dealer. He was the type that would just take whatever he wanted. He had a huge reputation in the community for taking things out of stores. He was barred from most stores in the neighborhood already. However, sometimes he would take a much smoother approach.

He would go in the store and say, "Hey, I'm so hungry, is there any way I can sweep or mop the floor just to make some extra money to buy something to eat." If the cashier at the store hadn't already heard about his reputation they would allow him to do that. Unfortunately, while he is in there sweeping, he would also be sweeping the store for whatever he wanted. We already knew by the time he would come out of the store he would have at least 7 or 8 items, some for himself, and some to sale.

One Saturday morning, as I set on the block of 43rd and Calumet selling my drugs he came on the block and told me he needed to hit a lick. I was thinking he was wanting to go steal something from the store as usual for some quick cash. It was a pretty slow day on the block for me as well, so I'm like sure I'll go be the lookout guy. So we went to the neighborhood store, but what I thought was very unusual this time is that he brought a gun with him. I thought nothing of it. 10 minutes of being outside I heard 2 very loud gunshots. I was like, "OH SNAP!" What has JR done? Thinking he had shot the store owner, Mr. Chin. I went inside to grab him, but when I ran in the store the first thing that I notice was JR., laying in a puddle of his own blood, shot in his forehead. Then Mr. Chin turned the gun at me thinking I was in on it. I left running, scared, confused and so hurt.

That was my first introduction to death. I have seen dead bodies before, but this was the first time I was actually with someone and within a matter of minutes they didn't even exist anymore. I then had to run back on the block and tell his sister's, brother and his mother, Ms. Rose, that her son was just murdered.

I watched her break down day after day until his funeral. I Couldn't help but blame myself for what happened to him. Every day I would think of what I could have done to make this not happen. When I saw that gun, I should have said something, or maybe I could have told him, not today, don't go to that store. Anything to keep him alive, but the reality was, I failed him.

For the first couple of months, It was hard for me to believe he was actually gone. To this day, I still think about him and what kind of man he would've become if only I would have stopped him that day.

Chapter 8

Getting Shot

In my 7th grade year, we moved to 79th & Loomis. This was an ok neighborhood, Chicago typical neighborhood. Gangs, drugs, violence, and shootings every night. This block was also owned by the gang, Gangster Disciples. We lived in a pretty decent duplex though with our landlord living underneath us. Her name was Miss Fitchell, she was about 65 years old with a son who had a disability.

I would bounce back & fourth on the CTA, (Chicago Transit Authority), from 79th to 43rd & Calumet going to school and still hitting the block for cash. My sister Angie and I went to this school called Cook Elementary on 81st in Bishop. So from 79th to 81 was Gangster Disciples, but from 82nd to 85th was another gang called Black Stones.

The Black Stones was our rivalry gang. Although I was plugged GD on 43rd & Calumet and had my membership over there, I still had a sense of duty over here since my neighborhood was also GD's. Plus by this time my sister had told me she had joined the gang

GD here on 79th known as "Killerward". So I told her I'm down with you guys.

Every day before, and after school, we would fight with the Black Stones. However, after school we would fight until the fight ended up back in one of our neighborhood's and the OG's (Older Gangsters) would get involved and bring out a gun and start shooting until someone got shot.

I had a good friend in my 7th Grade class named Dontae. He was a Black Stone and I was GD. Mrs. Nash didn't play that gang mess in her class. She had a well-respected son that was locked up and no-one messed with her. She was also a great teacher that loved all her students. Dontae and I started off to a very bad start when we first started class trying to fight. Mrs. Nash made us sit down and realize how much we had in common. Dontae & I became real cool in class, we would be cool but had to fight against each other before and after school. We always made it a point not to swing on each other but to just jump in and help our team fight someone else.

One day we had a plan for the Black Stones after school. We hid bricks & bottles on the block where we would usually fight on. As we backed them into their neighborhood their OG's came out shooting and one of our GD's was hit, his name was Dontario, he was in the 8th Grade, the same as my sister Angie.

As soon as he made it home from the hospital we all went over to his house to plan our revenge. My 7th grade teacher Mrs. Nash also came over to see him and saw all of us there plotting on something and told us to stay clear and let the police do their job. We didn't listen though, shortly after we planned our revenge attack. It was going according to plan, then I heard 10 shots, by the 5th shot, I felt something hard hit my chest. As we were running I remember squeezing my chest real hard trying to get out these short breaths. As we approached 79th my sister turned around and said, "B, you're hit!" I looked down and saw my green & white Adidas sweater covered in blood and fainted.

When I woke up in the Hospital the first face I remember seeing wasn't my mother or father, it was my teacher, Mrs. Nash and she had brought Dontae by to see me as well. When my mother did come to the Hospital I remember my mother and Mrs. Nash having a deep conversation. We had just recently heard about my sister getting pregnant by this older guy on the block named Kool-Aid. He was also plugged with our gang of GD's on 43rd & Calumet. She was 13 at this time and he was about 28.

Christine, my mother's friend, had moved her and her family to Montgomery AL, she had heard what was going on with us and decided to reach out to my mother. "Girl, what are you still doing in Chicago? These projects down South look like condos girl, you better come on down here and apply for the housing authority." That's just what my mother did. She left us in Chicago and went down South to apply and when she was approved she came back and said, "Ok, it's time to pack it up and moved down South." My sister and I were like "We are moving to where?" We were ready for some kind of change so we just decided to roll with it.

Chapter 9

The Move to Montgomery

The memories I have of Chicago – that city is a dog eat dog world. If you are weak, you will get crumbled. Only the strong survive. You have to go hard no matter what you do. There is no mediocre there. As soon as you wake up, you wonder "Who got killed last night? Whose house got broken into?" I know crack hit Oakland and Detroit hard, but it hit us in Chicago even harder. Kids were raising kids in the neighborhoods I lived in.

As soon as we got to Montgomery, AL I noticed everyone was super country. When we first got to Montgomery, I was thinking where are the horses and cows. I was very curious to know if white people were the same way in the South like I would see on the videos we would watch in school for Black History month.

My mom had a spot in Tulane Court. Christine lived over in Gibbs Village. It was easier for us to adapt there because they'd been in Montgomery for a couple of years. In Gibbs village, we had the Blue Boys, they were known for being a dangerous gang in the neighborhood. They were super cool and had some of the best parties ever. We reunited with Christine kids because they were our long-time friends growing up and decided to go to the school where they were going to school. So we went to school at McIntyre Middle School. I had different people tried to show me around. I was in the 8th grade, and Mr. Stewart was my teacher. I can remember that we had our first little dance on a Friday night. I had never been to a school dance after dark before because they were never going to do that in Chicago.

At the school dance, I was shocked, I had never seen all that booty shaking in my life! Even the thugs were dancing like that. It was a different culture. The girls in Montgomery took popping to a whole 'other level. Montgomery was different; I felt free. People weren't being killed every day. In 1996, there were only 11 or 12 murders that year. We felt safe coming from a place where there were a couple of hundred murders a year. You could walk anywhere in

Montgomery and not worry about who owned the block. In Chicago, you couldn't walk two blocks down the street without the gang changing and them wanting to beat you up or kill you.

In Montgomery though, I felt safe. However, I did feel like the school system was very behind. They were learning the things I'd learned in the 5th grade, in the 8th grade. I always felt like Montgomery was three steps behind. In my head, I was thinking I might have to kill these kids, but they were just thinking they wanted to have fun and wrestle with me.

Everyone around the school heard I was from Chicago, plus it didn't help our long-term friends had already had lots of beef with the people in the school Already. On my third day at the school, I got into my very first fight. Some guy made fun of my shoes. He said, "Are those the shoes y'all wear in Chicago cuz, we don't wear them kind of shoes down here", the class all laughed. What they didn't know is that with the attitude, I wasn't about to take no crap off of anyone.

So I hit him in the chin as hard as I could which knocked him back on his butt, that marked me.

The next Monday I got into another fight. By that Friday about 4 of them plan to jump me and we got into a huge brawl. My sister saw this brawl and she jumped in pregnant and all. They called us both to the office and expelled us. We ended up having to go to school over at Houston Hill since we lived in Tulane Court anyway.

Chapter 10

Alternative School

So now I was going to a new school in Montgomery called Houston Hill. There I ran into some of the same stuff, being the new kid on the block. Where students thinking they were about to bully me. They had no idea I wasn't about playing any games, or that I was coming from a place where you had to fight every day to survive. I made it in Houston Hill School for about 3 months and then I was put out of there as well for more fights. They just decided to expel me from the Montgomery Public Schools System all the way around.

I had to go to this alternative boot camp school call Project Upward. As soon as you get off the bus you have drill sergeants right in your face telling you where you needed to be and that was on the blacktop getting ready for morning PT. 7 am as soon as you got off the bus you were required to exercise, 100 jumping jacks, 50 dips, 50 pushups, 50 sit-ups, plus so much more. You had to walk with your hand behind your back on the campus at all times. You had to ask permission before you walked into any classroom, lunchroom, or bathroom and wait for someone to grant you that permission.

When I first got there I notice this one huge guy standing at about 6'2" 280 lb. all muscle, his name was Mr. Gavin. I also noticed a couple of guys called themselves trying to be tough and ran up on him to fight. I saw him dropping them on their backs, I mean he was knocking them out left and right. He would tell them, "If you want some, come get some", I was blown away. Like where am I? Then he came up to me like "Is your name, Charles Lee?" I was like, uuummmmmm (LoL).

He called me into his office and said, "Are you this Charles that I keep hearing about? That tough guy from Chicago that likes to fight and get into trouble?" I said, "Well my name is Charles." He said, "I know you think you are a tough guy and all, but around here we don't play that shit, around here I will knock your fat a## out. There's only one person around here in charge and that is me. You got that Jack?"

That was my first encounter with a male figure that was straight up with me in that manner. I was like whatever, I'm just here for 6 months so I can go back to school. After that, he would call me in his office and we would have long talks about what my future looked like. He would tell me, "Son you are not like these guys, you have greatness in you." It was like he could see something in me that I could never see. He became more of a mentor to me than anything.

We had a serenity prayer we had to say every day before lunch.

"God grant me that serenity to accept the things I cannot change, Courage to change the things I can, and the wisdom to know that difference, A quitter never wins, and a winner never quit, Sir."

I still say that to this day! The day I left that school, I told him thanks for being a role model to me. He told me, "Son, that's my job, now take what you've learned here and apply it to your life."

I can still remember getting my first Job at Churches Chicken. When I saw Mr. Gavin and his family walk in the door, I had never been so proud of someone to see me working. Although I was the cook, I told the cashier to step aside on this one, I wanted to take this order. He said, "Son, I'm so very proud of you. I was so proud of myself at that same moment.

Chapter 11

The Crew

So shortly after having to go back to Tulane Court, there was a guy that lived behind my apartment. He was about 300 lbs. and he would always be playing football with the younger guys out there. One day I walked up to him and asked, "What's your name bro?" He said, "They call me big Tony, what's your name?" From that day we became extremely tight. I mean we pretty much hung together all-day every day.

I tried to get him a job at Church's Chicken but for some reason, they wouldn't hire him so he found a job at Burger King. I applied to Burger King as well for my second job and I got it. Now, not only did we hang out together every day we also worked together. Every Friday and Saturday night we would go to buy matching outfits and then hit the club; we were pretty much inseparable.

Another young guy moved into the neighborhood, Tulane Court, his name was Curtis. Then it was 3 of us hanging out, then Curtis introduced us to his cousins Watski and Tasha. Then we added a couple more people to our circle. It was official, we had our crew. We worked hard and we played even harder. Although we were just 15 & 16 years old there was a club in West Montgomery on Mildred Street called, The Cabana Club, that would let us in to drink. We will go and get drunk off our butts, dance all night and have the best times ever!

As the year progressed, we started going to different clubs as well. I can still remember going to one club on the Southern Boulevard. It was the whole crew there that night and I had invited my sister and her friends. I told them there was no need for ID, I knew the bouncers that would let us in. We were having the best time ever until they played this song Ying Yang Twins, whistle while you twerk. The club was going crazy. Out of nowhere, we started hearing shots inside the club, machine guns.

As people were starting to run outside we noticed they were also shooting on the outside of the club. All you could see were bodies hitting the floor and people trampolining over other people to make it outside. When the shooting finally stopped I made sure that I found my sister first, and then my crew. We found everyone besides Curtis, that's when we begin to freak out.

They were not willing to let us back in the club due to all the bodies lying on the floor. So I begin to become aggressive for them to let me in so I could see if my homie was one of the people on the floor. One of the bouncers let me in, all I can remember was so much blood on that floor and people crying for their lives.

I started to yell, "Curt, Curt where are you, bro", he said, "I'm right here man." He hid in the bathroom while the shooting was taking place, but as he came out of the bathroom he noticed that it was money, drugs, black & mild's and jewelry all over the place so he decided to collect them. We were all concerned about him being alive, while he's still inside racking up on other people stuff (LoL). Till this day we are still all friends.

Chapter 12

Dating Older Women

I have always been pretty mature for my age. So when It came to dating girls I would always look for someone that was on my level of maturity or at least close to it. I've always found older women super attractive but being so young, I never gave it a shot until one day this lady called our home phone. She had the wrong phone number but she sounded like she was beautiful. Her name was Connie. I tried to hit her with as much charm as I could find to keep her on the phone. I don't know exactly what I said to keep her entertained for so long, but somehow that first conversation we stayed on the phone for 5 hours.

We then begin to talk daily until we finally agreed to meet up. She was 48 at the time and I was 15. But I lied and told her I was 22 because not only was I very mature for my age, I was also very big for my age, so she believed me. However, my mother got word of her age and when she would call our house my mother would be like; "What are you doing? You are the same age as me, and my son is only 15." She eventually figured out how old I was but at that time I think she was already catching feelings.

One night we had planned to take it to the next level. She paid for a hotel room and told me she would be there to pick me up around 9 p.m. I was like sweet! This would be my first time being intimate with an older woman. She came and got me as planned then we went to the hotel room.

Although I was super excited, I was also very nervous because I knew she had kids already and had been intimate with grown men so I didn't know if I would measure up. Oh well, we were here now so it was time to take it to the next level.

She performed oral on me and I can't lie it was the best I'd ever had thus far. Then she laid back for the reciprocation and I became extremely nervous because this would be my first time. As I attempted to go down on her, I got more nervous and nervous, the more I went down. As I got to her belly button I gave myself a little pep talk like; "Hey buddy, you can do this." As soon as I got to the promise land, and I was about to dive in, I freaked out and instead of putting my mouth there, I started rubbing my hair in her private part (LoL). I knew she was thinking in her head "What the hell are you doing? You're going to give me carpet burns (LoL)." She was so patient and understanding with me as she pulled me back up and showed me the proper way to do it.

We dated for about a year. It was pretty awesome. Next thing I knew my homie Big Tony was like, "Hey, we got a new lady at the rental office and since we know you like them granny's, I know you will love her because she is fine." However, that it would turn out being more of a challenge to get her to go out with me because I was so young.

I went to the office and let her know that I thought she was beautiful, and what my intentions were. She said, "How old are you." I said, "22" (LoL). She laughed and said, "Boy, I'm old enough to be your mother, that would never happen." I didn't let it stop me though. Every day I would go to the rent office with either a card, candy, or flowers, Trying to let her know I was not going to stop until she gave me a date. It took about 5 months to get her to agree to go on a date with me.

It was now game time. The first date went so well she agreed to go out with me again, and again. We made it a good 2 years and she spoiled me well in so many ways. Although I had never lived with her I would spend nights over there and weeks at a time. On Saturdays I would still hang with my crew to go out to the Cabana Club which was right around the corner from her house. It was really to the point where I fell in love with her, or so I thought. She told me that she felt the same way.

I went and brought her an engagement ring from JCPenney's ,it was only $10 but it looked like it was worth $10k. She was so happy and told all of her family. A couple of weeks later the diamonds began to fall out, she was so embarrassed and very hurt. That's when our relationship started to take a turn for the worse.

I would usually go over to her house after the club, but one particular Saturday I decided to go straight home. The next time I saw her she was so pissed off that I didn't come to her house, we got into a huge fight. That caused her to bust the windows out of my car and slash all four of my tires, and when I went to grab the knife she ended up stabbing me in my arm. After grabbing the knife I noticed that my hand was cut as well. I decided I couldn't put up with that anymore so we both agreed to call it quits.

I later saw this older lady working at the Churches Chicken up the street from my house. I thought she was super attractive so I started flirting with her. Her name was Jannise, she was about 47 at the time and I was about 17. It took me about 3 months before she and I were dating. She had 5 kids; 3 girls and 2 boys that were my age and a little younger. But of course, I had lied about my age. Just when we had gotten serious, I got the news about going to JOB CORPS!

Chapter 13

My Father

Returns

Just when my life starting to get on the right track, I got the news that my dad was coming to Montgomery, Alabama. I knew that his drug problem had gotten worse but at that time I just didn't know how bad it was. When he first got to Montgomery, Alabama, he stayed sober for about a month and a half and then it got BAD!

First, he would start stealing little things around the house. Then he started stealing bigger things around the house to the point that my friends would call me and say, "Hey B, I think your dad just stole your TV at your house." Then he would start stealing from other people's homes. And that would cause me to lose friends. When someone would break into their homes, they just assumed it was my dad.

He started shaking down my friends for change as they walked to school. Like, "You know my son, give me a quarter or 50 cents or something." As if that wasn't embarrassing enough, when my mom would put him out of the house he began sleeping in dumpsters around the neighborhood. So every day in school I would be the butt of someone's joke because of the actions my father decided to take.

He started to take my mother's car and pawned it for $20 to dealers for drugs. So now we would have to go and try to get my mother's car back from the dealers as she rode the bus until we could locate her car. It went downhill from there; he was stealing everything that wasn't nailed down.

I can remember going to sleep on Christmas Eve with presents under the tree and waking up to an empty tree. I also remember one night sleeping on top of my wallet just so he wouldn't steal it, only to wake up and notice my money and the wallet was gone. He promised me he didn't take it, even offered to help me look for it. The entire time we were looking for my wallet I knew in my heart that he took it but just wanted to believe that I would eventually find it. Well, weeks later he confessed to taking my wallet and money.

Things got to a point where he started stealing our socks, underwear and soap. One night I was fed up with it and I saw him walking out the house with our tissue and soap to go sell. I just had enough, so I decided to rush him, we got into a fight that night. I can remember after our fight me telling my mother something has to give, either he has to go, or I will go.

With so much going on at my house I would take my frustrations to school. My 11th-grade year I got into another huge fight at Robert E. Lee High School. After that fight, they took me to Air Base jail and my mother had to come to pick me up from there. Just like that, I was put out of the Montgomery Public Schools System yet again and had to go back to project upward for round 2. Mr. Gavin was still there, he was pretty disappointed at first, but as we talked he saw what I was facing at home.

When I got back to Robert E Lee during my senior year, they informed me that none of my credits from the project upward would count this time. And I would have to repeat the 11th grade. So the first day of my senior year was the day I dropped out of high school.

<u>Chapter 14</u>

Job Corps

With so much going on around my house I needed a way out, not just out of my apartment, but out of the city. So I applied for Job Corps in Gadsden Alabama. It took a couple of weeks for me to get the final approval but when they did respond, I was OUT! No looking back.

I can still remember getting there two weeks before the Christmas break. The first thing that I noticed was

1. This school looked like a college campus

2. They treated the white guys on the campus so bad.

I can still remember walking into the male dorm that evening and watching them ask this one white guy to come to the foyer of the building, they poured 3-week old milk all over him. He went back to his room in tears. I had no clue what the heck was going on but I felt really bad for him. The next day you could see everyone plotting on something. I saw everyone talking about it, I just didn't know the details. It was to beat up these four white guys that usually tried to stand up for themselves. So the next night in the hallway on the B wing hall of the dorm, all the guys from the A, C & D wing all came to the B wing hall to jump on these white guys. At least a hundred guys, I felt so bad for them I just went into my room and closed the door.

To my surprise the next morning I was called to the office to be terminated for being one of the guys that jumped on these white guys. I tried telling them, "Hey you're making a mistake, I had absolutely nothing to do with that." They said, "We are sending a lot of you guys home and then after we review the recorded footage, if you had nothing to do with it we will call you to come back. So just like that, I was back in Montgomery, back home trying to tell people that I had nothing to do with the reason why I got kicked out this time. Judging from my record though, no one believed me.

A week later I got a call from Job Corps letting me know they had reviewed all of the footage, the footage showed that I did return to my room and came out after the fight was done, so I was able to come back the next week. I was going there for my GED and also a trade. I decided to take Culinary Arts, being lazy. My trade choices were, Brick Masonry, Welding, Carpentry, Heating and Cooling HVAC. I was like, "Nope, I'm good on all of them, I'll just take Culinary Arts." I knew it would be some great eating there.

Although I was still dating Janise back home, I ended up meeting this young lady from New York named Mandy. She wasn't the prettiest girl on campus but she was one of the smartest and she dressed very well every day. That year, we both won people's choice for the best-dressed male and female on the campus. She also had a boyfriend on campus, his name was Ben, but somehow that didn't stop us from hooking up.

By this time I had become a mentor on the campus over the orientation classes. This means that when people first come to the campus I got the opportunity to show them around. So basically I had first dibs on all the ladies (LoL). One day in orientation class there were these two white young ladies that look like twins, both beautiful! We called them the double-mint twins but their names were Rachel and Mohona. Me and my roommate, Dollar Bill, both said we had to get one of them.

So I would show them around campus which lead to us becoming great friends and as well, gave us the opportunity to meet their mother. She thought I was funny. I assured their mom that I would keep a close eye out for them. Well, one day Rachel asked me if I wanted to go out, I was like sure whatever. Although I wanted the other sister I was still willing to settle for her, she was cool and cute. Now when we all came together they were always arguing for some reason. I was pretty confused until one day their roommate came to catch me up to speed and broke it all down to me. She said Charles, they both like you. I overheard Mohona telling Rachel that she liked you first.

Rachel and I dated for a short while, but after long I realized that we had very little in common, I would walk Mohona to most of her classes anyway. So one day she said, "Hey, I have something to tell you", I said, "What is it", she said, "I liked you this whole time but my sister came for you first." I took the opportunity to let her know how I really felt. So I told her, "To be honest with you, I like you to, and I'm not feeling your sister." We sat at the cafeteria outside and talked for about 3 hours after that. Then we started to kiss. After we were done kissing we looked up and straight ahead was Rachel, staring at us. Then it started pouring down raining (LoL).

Rachel went home that weekend and Mohona stayed with me. This was one of the best weekends of my life. From Friday to Sunday we spent every minute together until we had to go to the dorms for curfew. That Saturday we went to see "Save The Last Dance" at the dollar movie. This movie was about a white young lady falling in love with a black male from the inter-city through dance.

We shared so many intimate details about our pass lives and the things that we had been through. She completely stole my heart that weekend. Only to find out that when Rachel went home that weekend she told her parents that Mohona was doing the ultimate No No! Dating a black guy! She conveniently forgot to mention to them that she and I were dating first (LoL). I had no clue how they felt about black people, but boy was I in for a rude awakening.

The Next Monday morning her mom was at the school withdrawing her from the Job Corps program. I was so sad. Although they pulled Mohona out, for some reason they let Rachel stay in the program. I wanted nothing to do with her because she had everything to do with Mohona leaving school.

By this point, I was just about completed with the program. I had received my GED and finished my trade-in Culinary Arts. I was just waiting on Graduation to receive my money for completing. I had become very angry because my communication with Mohona was over.

One night a young man came into my room and ate my chips from my locker. As soon as I came into my room, my roommate told me what happened. Usually, I could look over stuff like this, but I needed a place to take out my frustration and he granted me that opportunity. I went to his room, lock the door so no one could get in or out and I gave him a pretty good beat down. Then I left his room. Shortly thereafter a couple of people came by my room and asked me what did I do to him. He had knots all over his head.

As I was sleeping that morning, the head of the school came to wake me up at about 5 am and informed me that he saw the bruises on the guy's face, I had to leave the campus that day. But the great news was I would get my $1,200 early and not have to go to graduation to get it. They gave me my money and before I left Gadsden, Alabama one of the mentors took me car shopping. I was able to buy an all-white 98

Mitsubishi Galant. Now with my car, I drove away from job corps, right back to Montgomery, Al.

Chapter 15

Love of my Life

Shortly after I left school, I got a call from Mohona, that was the best call of my life! She explained to me all of the racial things that she was going through by falling in love with a black guy. She explained to me that her parents weren't fond of black people by no means, and they said that they would never let her speak to me again. She would go to her friend's house to call me, even if that meant her sneaking her parent's car to do so. Hanging up the phone was so hard to do because we never knew when we would speak again.

One day as she was sneaking the car to ride to a friend's house to call me, she got into a car wreck. She called me and said, "I just wrecked my mom's new car, I don't know what I should do." I told her whatever she needed me to do, I would do. She then told me that her father had put a gun to her head one night and said, "I will kill you before I let a nigger, have you." I said, "Grab your stuff, I'm on my way."

It was about 8 pm and I rode up there to pick up the love of my life. We came back to Montgomery. I was just about to turn 18 and she was 17, turning 18 soon. Neither one of us had ever lived on our own so far, we were kind of lost when it came to our next step. As long as we were together though, we were just fine.

We went to this hotel you can pay for by the week, we stayed there for about 2 months until we could save up enough money for our first apartment. The whole time I was getting calls from her parents, with her dad saying, "You F###ing Nigger, I'm going to blow your brains out when I see you." At this point me and her father had never met each other face to face before, so I would say, "Sir, I can walk right past you today and you would never know who I was because you've never taken the time to meet me, please call me back when you have something positive to say." (LoL) The bad thing was she had always told me how much she loved her dad and how close their relationship was. I felt like I was the one breaking them apart.

I got a new job working at the Olive Garden in Montgomery, AL serving tables. We saved up enough money to finally get a place. We moved into some apartments called the Palisades. Our first night we had no blankets, pillows, furniture, or anything, we just slept on our bags of clothes with our coats as our covers. We had each other and that was all that mattered.

We made our way to Rent-A-Center very shortly after. For some great rent-to-own furniture. The Palisades was the ghetto, we had an empty pool with no water, and every time Mohona went to the apartment laundry room she had to take the gun with her. Our apartment ended up getting broken into on two separate occasions, it was then time for us to go.

We found a place at Three Fountains. About this time her parents were still not speaking to her. So I asked her, "If your family doesn't want to have anything to do with you, will you be a part of my family?" The next morning before we went to church I had already called my family and the Pastor to let them know I was proposing to Mohona that day. So by the end of service, the Pastor asked if Mohona and I would come to the front, that was my time to shine.

I had written the sweetest poem ever and had all of my nieces and nephews to help with it. Such as, every time I would say you are my rose, they would bring her a rose, or call her my queen they brought her a crown. When I said, "You are so sweet", they would bring candy. To finish it all off, my youngest nephew brought out the ring and I asked her for her hand in marriage. We went to the courthouse to get married the next day! This was April 2001 and we were both 18 and ready to leave Montgomery. We pulled out a map and closed our eyes and said, "Where are we going next." Our fingers landed on Florida.

Chapter 16

Moved to Florida

After being in Montgomery for a year we decided it was time for a change. So I asked Mohona, "Where do you want to move to?" She said, "I don't know, where would you like to move to?" So we got a map out, closed our eyes, put our hands together and just put our fingers on a spot and said, "We are going there!" This place happened to be Florida.

I just recently worked with a guy at Olive Garden named Charles as well, he just so happened to have moved to Florida. I reached out to him and told him that we were trying to move to Florida and asked if there was any way we could come to visit to see what it was like there, he said, "Sure." So the next week we decided to take a week's vacation to see if we would like it and if we could find an apartment there. We found this gorgeous apartment that we fell in love with, it was called Willowick's.

We completed the application, got approved and we packed up our stuff and moved within a month. We moved there and fell in love. It was so different from

Montgomery and Chicago. So many happy people, I just figured everyone was so happy there because no matter where they worked, even if they worked at McDonald's, they knew at the end of their shift they could always go to the beach for free.

My family would always love to come to visit, plus it didn't hurt that our place was right on top of the pool. We met awesome friends and we went to some of the best night clubs Pensacola had to offer. One day I was approached in the club by a stranger. He said, "Man you have a beautiful wife, what do you do for a living." I told him that I was just a hard-working man just like he was. He said, "Man we have parties once a month at my house I would love for you guys to come." I said, "Yeah sure, maybe one day we can get up that way."

Well, about 2 weeks had past then I ran into him again at the same night club. He said, "We are having a party tomorrow, I would love you to come." So he gave us the address and we talked about going but then we though, maybe not. We ended up going out to dinner, had some drinks and then we figured hey, why not, let's try the party out. As we approached the party we noticed that this gated house was huge! It was on the water, and about four stories high, that's how it looked from the outside.

So we went into the party, and the first thing that we noticed was that everyone at this party was dressed sexy. After walking around about 10 minutes we ran into the host of the party, he was so happy to see us, he said "I'm glad you guys made it out." He showed us around and then informed us what kind of party this was. He let us know that this was a swingers party. I had never even heard of a swinger's party so he had to break it down to me. He said, "This is a party of open-minded couples that like to share partners." I was like, "WTF, is this why you asked us to come?" He said, No not really, I have these parties once a month and for these parties I would like to provide the drugs. I was wondering if there's any way you can get me a kilo of cocaine for these parties."

He told me that the last guy that used to provide the drugs for his parties he gave him $30,000 for a kilo and asked was that something I would be interested in. I told him that I would think about it. A couple of days later I reached out to one of the guys there I knew sold cocaine. I asked him, "Hey, do you think you could get your hands on a kilo of cocaine and how much would it cost me? He replied, "Yes, I can, the price would be $20,000.

I reached back out to the guy that had the parties and I told him it was a go. The very first party he gave me $30,000 to go get the drugs. Something in my mind said take this 30,000 and run, but then another voice in my head said if he could afford to give you $30,000 he could probably afford to give someone else $50,000 to come to hunt you down. So I just did the right thing and brought his drugs back. Not to mention I made $10,000 on that one transaction.

They were pretty impressed with the drugs I brought for the party, so I became the regular guy. I begin to notice when I brought the drugs no one would weigh it out, they would just open up the bag and start getting high. So I started being greedy, as if I wasn't already making enough money. I started by taking one ounce of the cocaine out of his package, then two ounces, then three.

No one cared as long as the drugs were good. I would take the drugs that I had broken down into 8-balls and quarters to sell them on the beach. All of these rich people on the beach would pay top money for drugs so they didn't have to ride back over the bridge in the hood to look for it, I was their guy. I would sale them an 8-ball for $450 when it usually goes for $150. But the drugs I was getting were very good quality.

Once the ecstasy pills came on the scene everyone wanted them as well, especially my guy that threw the parties. He wanted 500 at a time so I was charging him $20 a pill and I was paying $10 a pill; you do the math (LoL).

Slowly I became the man in the city. A young guy that could get my hands on any drugs in the city. Now every night club that we went to would already know that I was the man with the great cocaine and ecstasy pills. They would already have our seats at the bar waiting for us. This was the good life, or so I thought!

Chapter 17

Headed to Jail

So I was the man in Pensacola. The guy that I was supplying for with the parties was very connected in Pensacola, plus I was making connections of my own. The San Shaker on the beach was a very popular place for Doctors, Lawyers, Judges, and Business Owners that all wanted good cocaine but didn't want to drive back across that bridge to get it. Everyone was very excited when I showed up.

On a good Saturday on the beach, I would make about 7 grand. At 19 years old I wasn't a very good steward over my money, but we were living the best life. Super nice crib that we didn't own, and nice luxury vehicles. We took trips twice a month, Jamaica, Mexico, the Bahamas, and all over the USA. My two nephews got the opportunity to come live with us and we were able to spoil them rotten. Nice clothes, Jordan's, plus we got to take them on family trips as well. It was a great breath of fresh air for them. As well, whatever my family back in Montgomery needed, I was able to cover them.

Mohona's brother came to Florida to live with us seeking new opportunities. He had been painting in their family business since he was young. However, when he came to Florida it was hard for him to find steady work. I needed a way to account for all of the extra cash that I was making, so I suggested to him for us to start a painting business of our own. He thought that was a great idea and agreed. We started a painting business called, Jones and Lee painting. He mostly did all of the work, I was just the money guy.

My father came to live with us in Florida as well, seeking a better opportunity to straighten out his life, we put him on the paint crew as well. Everything was going just right! My family came down for a visit one weekend, and as they were approaching town my guy called and asked if I could score him one because they decided to have a last-minute party. So, of course, I said yes.

As soon as my connection dropped off the package, my family showed up not giving me enough time to go drop off the package. As soon as they came I greeted them and said I have to make a run really quick. The only thing I noticed before I left was my sister going into my bedroom.

When I came back my sister was still in my bedroom but she was crying. I asked what was wrong but she never would tell me. For the entire weekend that they were there, she was just acting really strange. The rest of us went out on that Saturday night, she opted out of going. She continued to act strange until they left but never told me why.

On their drive back home my other sister called me and said, "Hey, I want to tell you why Angie was acting so strange, the devil is trying to take your life." I just blew it off and said, "Isn't that his job, to try and take our life?" She said, "Take it however you want but I'm just relaying the message."

So just like I normally do when I would take him his package I would normally take out about 2 or 3 ounces and about 30 to 40 pills. So the next weekend after they left it was time for me to make my beach run. I got dressed, rolled me up a couple of blunts, and headed to the beach. While on my way to the beach a customer called and asked me if I could bring them a quarter to this spot called Gene's Lounge, another notorious spot for drug users. I made lots of money there too. I had to keep regular prices there because it was in the city limits. I stopped there & served him and now I was headed to the beach.

I fired me one up for the road and as soon as I took about five puffs I went up this hill and as I was coming down there was a roadblock set up and all I could see were officers. My car was full of smoke and I heard the officer say, "Roll down your window." I was like, "But I don't want to (LoL)." They circled the car and as I rolled down the window, so much smoke came out of the car. They said, "Sir, pull over out of the street and step out." As soon as I was trying to pull over I started trying to hide the drugs everywhere but it didn't work. As soon as I got out of the car they started patting me down and the cocaine fell right out.

I had stuff the ecstasy pills in my butt only because at that time they were trying to charge you with a felony for ecstasy pills. They put me in the police car because of the cocaine and marijuana. As I was in the back seat of the police car I laid on my side trying to get the ecstasy pills out before I got to the police station. The officer saw me and said, "Boy, what are you doing?, If you have anything else you might as well just tell me now so you don't get contrabanded once you go to the station." For a second I thought about telling him the truth but then I was like they will just have to find it.

As I got in the police station they begin to process me, I was so scared because I knew it was just a matter of time before those pills fell out. They brought me in, searched me down and to my surprise the pills never came out. As I made it upstairs I checked inside my butt and they were not there either. I just counted that as a great blessing from God.

I called my wife and told her that I had gotten arrested. She called up one of our good friends, Regina, and she came and bonded me out, she put up her house for me. In the state of Florida, you have to go to court in 2 weeks to plead innocent or guilty, they call that arraignment. Well, the night before two weeks arraignment, my buddy called again and wanted me to score for his party. I knew I had tons of legal fees ahead so I knew I needed to go get this money.

My regular guy that I usually would score from was out of town so I called up another guy that usually dealt in lighter weight. I asked him if he could get his hands on a kilo of cocaine. He told me he would make a couple of calls and call me right back. He called me back and said that he found one then came to pick me up so we could go and get it.

The next thing I know we pulled up to this deserted car wash which was Dark. This guy pulled up in front of us with the drugs. Trusting him with the cash I told him that he could go and grab it while I stayed back. I gave him the money to go grab it from his buddy in the car in front of us. As he went and got in the back seat I could see a couple of guys coming from behind the other side of the car wash in all black charging to the car.

I saw one of them pull out a gun and pointed it at the driver, then I could see the other guy on the passenger side pull out his gun and hit the guy on the passenger side in the face with the gun. I could see them take the drugs and the money and started running off. At this time I was calling my brother-in-law to tell him to go in my closet and bring me my gun. We all left that spot and headed to Whataburger to talk things over.

In the back of my mind, I knew that this was all planned, because how else would these robbers know exactly what time we would be there. As we pulled up to Whataburger my brother-in-law showed up with my gun. I told the guys that got robbed that they owed me because I knew that this was staged. They promised me that it wasn't but I didn't believe them. I told them I was taking everything in their car, TV's, headrest, speakers, amp, and they had a couple of pounds of weed in there as well. Ironic how the robbers didn't get that.

It took us a little while to get the stuff out of their car, but eventually we did. As we had everything loaded up and we were pulling off, the driver from the other car stops me and told me that this was fucked up how they got robbed now I was robbing them too. I told the guy that brought me there to stop the car, I got out and told him, "Brother, I'm not robbing you, I just cannot take a loss right now. Whenever you get my drugs or money this stuff is yours and I will not pawn it or sell it." As soon as I got that out of my mouth, all I could hear it was freeze put your hands up.

It was an undercover in a Ford Escort. I still had the gun in my pocket and was thinking of a way to get it off of me. He said loudly again, "Freeze mother F#####!" I was thinking to myself that maybe I could just faint and then when I hit the ground I could throw the gun under the car. He said, "This is my last time telling you to freeze or I will blow your brains out." After he said that, back up arrived.

They all jumped out with guns drawn, I put my hands up and they rushed me. After he patted me down, the officer yelled, "He has a gun!" Then they put me in the car first. I could see the officers talking to the rest of the guys out there for about 10 minutes, then they started searching their cars. Everyone started getting in the back of cars. The only person that didn't get arrested that night was my brother-in-law.

Once we all got to the station. I asked them how they got locked up too. Well, the guy from the other car stated the police asked him was I robbing him and he said no. Then the police said to him, "Yes, he's robbing you because all of your stuff from this car is in the car next to you." He said, "Officer, I just owed him some money, he was not robbing me." Then the police told him fine, they would just search his car and after that he would be free to go. However, the police found lots of sprinkles of cocaine and ecstasy pills all over the car from the guys that robbed them early, they were pretty clumsy and got the drugs everywhere. They then searched my buddy's car and found the two pounds of marijuana that we took from their car, so he went down for that. Now I have to call Mohona once again to let her know that I was arrested again.

I had court in the morning, so I needed to get out pretty quickly. Mohona called our friend Regina again and once again she came to bond me out, I was so embarrassed. When I got home I called my oldest sister and told her everything that was happening. I asked her, "Why do you think the monkey is on my back like this?" She said, "Do you remember when Angie said the devil was trying to take your life, it may be because of everyone's prayers that this was the Lord's way of slowing you down so the devil won't take your life." I hired a lawyer and begin the next fight of my life, for my life.

They were trying to pen a robbery charge on me. Around this time, they were trying to enforce stricter gun laws known as the, "10-20-LIFE", law. If in the act of committing a crime with a firearm, your sentence could hold 10 years. And if the gun was to be fired while a crime was being committed it could hold up to 20 years. If someone was shot while committing a crime it could be a life sentence. So with the two felonies, the DA came to me first with 10 years trying to scare me with this robbery charge. It freaked me out at first because I had never been to prison before. My lawyer seemed pretty confident with my case so I didn't accept it.

Every time I would have a really fun night out, as soon as I would ride pass downtown close by that courthouse I was reminded that my life was about to change drastically. My nephews would always try to encourage me and let me know that everything was going to be okay, but I never let them know how big of trouble I was in.

Going back and forth to court, I was getting pretty scared that I may have to do these 10 years. Thinking back on the conversation I had with my sister, I asked God, "Hey if you're up there I could use your help because there's no way I could do this alone." Out of nowhere I heard a small but strong voice that said: "I got you!"

The DA was pushing for these 10 years, but they could never get the guy to testify to robbery so they had to drop it to a concealed weapons charge which carried a much lighter sentence. Along with the possession charge, and marijuana, I was sentenced to give the system 2 years of my life. This was including jail and probation.

Chapter 18

My Jail

Experience

After agreeing to my sentence, the judge allowed me to go home for a week and to come back and turn myself in to start serving my sentence. That was the longest week of my life. I was grateful for the opportunity to get my nephew's situated and sent back home and also some good quality time to spend with my wife and close friends. I had to make sure that I was able to set my wife up before I left. I gave Mohona all of the money I had been saving up, a little over $30,000.

The day had come for me to turn myself in to start serving my sentence. As we drove to the courthouse Mohona was crying hysterically. She offered to walk me in, but I declined. We prayed and then I gave her a goodbye kiss and walked in the courthouse. I was off to the county jail.

When I first got to the County Jail I found me a bible and begin to read. My relationship with God was so new, but it felt so real. One day as I was reading the Bible and my roommate suggested to me that I should talk to this guy, he's known as the preacher man around here. I found preacher man and begin to talk to him. He told me a lot of great things that I agreed with, but then he hit me with something I wasn't ready for.

He said, "Do you know when I give God my best praise", I said, "No, please tell." He said, "After I have smoked me a joint." I laughed so hard, then I called him a fake. I then went back and told my roommate along with a couple of other guys that he was a fake preacher. That didn't stop me from reading my word and praying every night. I even started going to the devotions they had in there. After preacher man left, they allowed me to lead the prayer in our pods before lights out.

It was time to leave the county jail headed to the county road prison which was a work camp. When I first got there I instantly noticed things were so much different there, the food was even better. There were a lot of crazy things going on like fighting's, stabbings, and homosexuality. My goal was just to stay clear of all of that and remain focused.

While I was there my relationship with God became stronger. I began to ask God what my purpose was for being here, why was I created? God, why was my childhood so messed up? He spoke to me and said, "Son, I have a bigger purpose for you, once you get out of here, I need you to reach as many youth as you can, to redirect their life so that they won't make the same mistakes you made, so they don't end up in the same place you're in." I then understood.

The more I prayed the more visions he would give me. As I would lay on my rack he would begin to show me a place with a lot of kids running in and out. This place was colorful and had lots of different murals all over it. It had a restaurant there that teenagers were in charge of. It also had a dance studio, an education room and so much more. This was so awesome!

However, I was thinking to myself, where would we put something like this, Davis Highway, Pensacola Boulevard, the Scenic highway? Then God said, "No, you're going back to Montgomery, Alabama." I said the devil is a liar (LoL). I thought the devil was coming to confuse me because God knew how much I hated Montgomery, Alabama and that I never wanted to go back.

The very next morning I called Mohona, just like I did pretty much every morning, but before I could say anything she said, "Baby I had this weird dream!" I asked her what the dream about and she told me the dream was that we moved back to Montgomery, Alabama. So at that point, I knew it was God. However, I still couldn't get over the fact I hated it Montgomery, Alabama.

Once I was released, I was 80% sure that I needed to go to back to Montgomery, Alabama and 20% sure that it was something I really did not want to do. I checked in with my probation officer and she let me know all the rules and everything that could get me sent right back to jail. She also let me know that she was very strict and would not hesitate to send me back.

As well, she informed me that I will not be able to get my driver's license back until the next year.

I was only out for 3 days before my buddy that put on the parties gave me a call. He said, "I heard you're home, ready to make some money?" But what he didn't know, I made a promise to God that I would never go back to that lifestyle. He came to visit me at my home and I told him about my lifestyle change, he told me that he was proud of me and asked me if I could do them this one last favor. He even offered to pay me a bonus this time, not knowing that I was making 10 grand off the deal anyway. It was at that moment I knew I needed to leave Pensacola because I was falling back into the same trap that got me locked up in the first place.

Mohona came in right as he were leaving and asked me what we were talking about. I told her and she instantly started packing up all of our things to move back to Montgomery, Alabama. I still had doubts about moving back to Montgomery, Alabama but she gave me an ultimatum, either we leave, or she leaves. I knew I couldn't live life without her so I called my mother and let her know that we were coming back to Montgomery, Alabama. She was overjoyed and told me that we could live with her until we could find a place. Just like that, we were back in Montgomery, Alabama.

Chapter 19

Moving back to Montgomery

Once we got back to Montgomery, Alabama we shacked up with my mother. She lived in a neighborhood called Chisholm. I was kind of down that I move back to Montgomery, Alabama, so I spent the first two weeks just moping in self-pity. Then I got a job back at the Olive Garden there in Montgomery.

After two months of staying with my mother, my wife told me that it was time we found us a place. So she started searching for a home in the same neighborhood close to my mother in Chisholm. We found two homes that she loved and I met with the realtor so we could make a decision. The one in which we decided on had an awesome man cave in the back with a pool table and all kinds of good stuff. We bought it and now we were residents of the Chisholm neighborhood. I told God, "Hey, I'm here back in Montgomery now what would you like for me to do?" He said, "My son, now it's time for you to get to work."

When I got back to Montgomery, Alabama I had 13 nieces, nephews and little cousins. So I asked them what they were up to these days. Two of my nephews told me that they played basketball at the Chisholm Community Center and the rest of them were up to nothing at the time. So I went down to the Chisholm community center and spoke with the director there, his name was Mr. Jonathan. I told him that I was new to the area and I had two nephews that played basketball on his team there and I wanted to get involved. He let me know that they could really use some coaches. "Where do I sign up", I said.

With my other nieces and nephews, I started a dance team. The majority of them were excited about the idea but the rest, not so much. They did it because I was their favorite uncle. I got pretty deep into coaching basketball and as I was really starting to love it, God reminded me of the vision he gave me while I was locked up.

There was this really smart girl working at Olive Garden with me named Adrian. She was also doing some paralegal work at the time. I asked her was there any way she could help me out with a business plan. She asked me what kind of business it would be and I told her it was for a youth center, so she agreed.

I went over to her house one evening to start working on the business plan, I started telling her the whole vision room by room as detailed as I could possibly be. As she was writing down the vision room by room, she was also breaking down a budget for each room. Once she finished with the budget it ended up being about $380,000. She turned to me and asked where I was going to get this much money from. All I could say was, "God!" She said, "God is good and all, but don't you think you are putting a little too much on him?" I looked her right in the eyes and said, "Nope, this is what he put on my heart." So we continue and she asked me what was I going to name it, I said, "The Spot".

Chapter 20

Laurali

So now life in Montgomery was going great. I was coaching basketball, working at Olive Garden, had a nice little dance team where we were getting to perform at different churches and weddings and my wife's family was back to speaking to us. However, at this point, I still had not met her father face to face.

Her mom asked me if I would come down for a weekend and I told my mother but she told me not to do it. She said it's a setup, they're going to try and hang you (LoL). I agreed to go down for the weekend but I took my gun with me. I slept with it under my leg the entire time. We hit it off pretty good, we ate as a family and even played some board games. Believe it or not, they even invited me back.

I started coming down on a regular basis and we were getting along pretty good. I went to her father after about a year of me coming down and I asked him, "Are you ready now to walk your daughter down the aisle." He said, "Yeah, sure." I begin to plan a wedding on the beach. I wasn't 100% sure if he would back out last minute so I never told Mohona about this wedding. My sister and I went to pick out a wedding dress for Mohona, and I got her and my family rooms on the beach. The entire time she had no clue that our families were at the beach.

Then next morning we woke up and I gave her a white dress to put on, I was dressed in all white, and our friend showed up wearing all white, then the all-white limousine drove up to get us. She got curious and asked what was going on, we told her we were going to a nice all-white party.

As we pulled up on the beach, we parked and her father opens up the door and said, "Are you ready for me to walk you down the aisle?" I had never seen her cry so much. All of our family and close friends were there in all white on this beautiful white sand. We released 2 white doves and white balloons; it was so beautiful, not to mention this was our family's first time meeting each other.

Everything was perfect. We had everything we could hope for, the only thing that was missing was a child. So we did a 7-day fast for a child. Mohona's sister gave her a call to tell her they were taking her to jail and were taking her baby girl from her. She asked her if she could please help. Mohona turns to me and said, "What should we do?" I said, "Let's help."

As we were headed to get the child, Mohona's mother informed us that she was going to get the baby and we didn't have to worry about getting her. Well, after Mohona's mother had her for some months, we got a call from Mohona's sister again informing us that her mother had dropped Laurali off at DHR with her bags and just left her there. She asked again if there was any way we could help before they put her up for adoption and the family would never be able to see her again. We went to DHR the next morning trying to get custody of our niece.

Her caseworker said, "I asked your mother was there anyone else who could take her before dropping her back off here and she said no and judging from the way this family has treated this baby girl, whoever wants her, will have to get a lawyer and fight me for her." The next day we got a lawyer to do just that, fight for her. It took us 1 year of fighting and 6 different foster homes to finally get the judge to grant us guardianship!

She came to our house right before Christmas. We spent $5,000 that year for her Christmas trying to make her feel as comfortable as possible. She was just about to turn 4 around that time. When she turned 5, we signed her up for school at Dalriada in Montgomery, Alabama. She had a pretty difficult time adjusting to school because everyone would ask her who that black guy was picking and dropping her off to school. She would just say "That's my uncle", but you know how kids can be, they would ask her "How?"

Her Teachers, Counselor, and the Principal all knew what was going on but the students just never got it. That caused Laurali to be very upset to the point which she didn't want to go back to school. When I would pick her up she would run to the car fast so no one could see her walking with me.

About the time she made it to the third grade she got used to it and so were the kids in the school. She would always ask us about her mom and dad and why she didn't have them like the other kids in her school. One day she called us in her room and said, "Can I make a deal with you guys? If you guys would call me ladybug, I will call you guys mom and dad." We all cried at that moment and said, "Deal."

Just like that, God had blessed us with our first baby girl. I can remember about 5 years later, I asked God, "Whatever happened to what I fasted for, you know a child?" And then Laurali came and said, "Dad, can I go outside?" I was like, ok God, I understand! She has been the Joy of our lives ever since.

Chapter 21

Starting a

Mentoring

Program

We were new parents now which was so different from our typical lifestyle, we were trying to navigate through it. On top of that I had ventured off into helping to coach football with the Montgomery Chiefs, then baseball with the Montgomery Metro League. However, basketball was my core sport.

All of these spots where being offered in my neighborhood and by coaching sports, I thought I was doing what God had called me to do, working with these youth to keep them off of the streets, giving them something productive to do.

Within my fourth year of coaching basketball, it was my first day of warm-ups, I had a young man come in on my 11-12-year-old team with 2 tattoos, one on each arm. My first thoughts were what kind of parents allows an 11-year-old to get tattoos! However, as I thought on it more, I thought maybe at 11 years old he had parents like I had.

So I monitored him pretty closely and he did a really good job in the first couple weeks of practice, then he stopped showing up. I asked the team, "Hey, has anyone seen Nendo?" They said, "Coach, you haven't heard, Nendo's brother was killed last week trying to rob someone." That instantly broke my heart. I tried calling the number on his paperwork but it was disconnected.

He eventually came back to practice about 4 days after that. He came in right before practice and said, "Coach can you come outside really quick", I knew something was on his heart and I thought he wanted to talk to me about his brother. When I got outside he lifted his shirt and I saw a 45-caliber gun. He said, "Coach, where can I hide this at, I don't want to bring it in and disrespect the gym like that?" I tried not to act too surprised so I showed him a hiding place to put it. I told him after practice I was taking him home so I could talk to him and his parents.

As he came back in all of the other players welcomed him and embraced him with hugs and handshakes and said welcome back. After practice he got his gun and got in the car with me. As we begin to ride to his house I asked him, "Man, what are you doing with this gun?" He said, "Coach, you will never understand what I go through here in these streets." I looked him right in his eyes and told him, "You would be very surprised at what I could understand."

Then we spoke a little bit just about how he felt unsafe and he didn't want to end up dead like his brother. I assured him that the way he ends up dead is by putting himself in positions with guns. He said, "Coach, I promise I'm not trying to hurt anybody I just want to live." By this time we made it to his house and as he knocked on the door you could hear a group of guys in the living room saying stuff like who is that, put this up, put that up. He told them who he was and they opened the door.

As he went to the back in search of his mother, I peeked my head in the door and I could see drugs on the table being sorted out for sale, and some huge guns underneath the table, everyone in there were smoking marijuana. He came back and said, "Coach, my mother is not here, but can you talk to my auntie?" She was about 18 or 19 years old.

I informed her that I was the coach over at Chisholm and I needed to speak to his mother regarding his birth certificate before our first game, and a couple of other things. As I was talking to her, a couple of the other guys that was sitting down on the couch came up and started groping her as if I was hitting on her or something. They said to me, "Nigga what you need, you got some money or something?" I told them no, I was just a coach over at Chisholm and was trying to talk with his mother.

They got more ignorant and aggressive so I told his auntie I was about to leave but whenever his mother comes home to please have her give me a call. As I was leaving to walk to my car, I heard a loud yell saying, "Coach, please don't leave me here, these were the same guys that were with my brother when he got killed, they had guns and everything and they let him die on the street coach, please take me with you!" I thought for a second about what to do. Pondering, that it was probably not a good idea to take him with me. Should I call the police or DHR? Those actions more than likely wouldn't lead him to a better life.

It was so many questions going through my mind, and with him sitting on the porch waiting for my answer, I just got in my car and broke down. I started crying hysterically, asking God why did He put me in this position. What could I do to help him? God then reminded me of a promise that I made as I was locked up, He was showing me my purpose.

I did a lot of reflection on JR, knowing he died at 12 years old, he would never get an opportunity to see anything other than the southside of Chicago, never experience the life of having a wife and kids, that he would never meet my wife and kids. I made a promise that if I can ever change another young person's life, I wouldn't hesitate one moment. So I rolled down my window and let him know that I would be back tomorrow. With a very low voice he said, "Okay coach."

I went home that night and got on my hands and knees and prayed to God for direction. He showed me the vision again of a mentoring program. He said, "Instead of you teaching a young man how to win a basketball game, teach them how to win in life!" I said, "God, exactly how do I do that? I have no high school diploma; two felonies and I work at Olive Garden, what else can I do?" I thought I was doing exactly what He wanted me to do by coaching these young men, but I what never knew was that I had players dying emotionally every day. He said, "Start a mentoring program outside of coaching sports."

So that next morning I told my wife that I was starting a mentoring program. I picked up Nendo the next morning for school and asked to speak with his mother, but again she was not there. I told him on the way to school that I was starting a mentoring program and I would love for him to be my very first mentee. He said, "Sorry coach for acting like that last night, sometimes I just feel lonely and afraid and need someone to talk to." I let him know there was no need to feel sorry, and that's exactly what a mentor is, someone you can talk to about anything.

I asked him for suggestions for names for our new mentoring group. We came up with TOYB (Taking Our Youth Back). Every morning I would do my best to take him to school and pick him up. We would then work a little bit on the mentoring program before basketball practice. That year we went to the championship! I had finally started walking in my calling, other than teaching youth sports

Chapter 22

That's

My

Dog

Now that we had started the mentoring program, I had the opportunity to hang out daily with Nendo, except the days I would have to work at Olive Garden which was a lot. At this time, we had about 15 other students in our Mentoring Program. The only issue was every time that I would schedule an evening with the mentoring group I would be scheduled to work. I went to management and discussed with them that I had started a Mentoring Program, which they were very excited about the idea, just not excited enough to give me the time off that I needed.

So I decided to talk to my God again. If this is really what I'm supposed to be doing, can you please speak to my managers (LoL). Or better yet you can give me something of my own! I could hear him so clearly say, "What about a Hot Dog Cart? You've seen lots of them in Chicago, do you see any here?" I was like, "Nope!" He said, "Give it a shot!"

So I called my family all together and told them we are going to start a Hot Dog Stand business, everyone was on board and excited! The next morning I called down to the city of Montgomery on 25th and Washington and spoke with the person over the business licenses. I told him what I wanted to do regarding starting a Hot Dog Stand in downtown Montgomery. I could hear him laughing and then he said, "Young man, that will never happen. That is not the direction we are headed in the city of Montgomery."

Just like that, my dreams were killed! I gathered my family back up just to let them know that the Hot Dog business was a no go. I could see lots of disappointment on each of their faces. So instead of being defeated myself, I decided to use those looks on their faces as Motivation! I began to go to the County Commission, the City Council, and the Mayor, I asked why was this the case. They would all tell me that what I was told was never the case and from their knowledge, there was a possibility of someone starting a Hot Dog Stand.

So I took that information right back down to 25th and Washington. There was a very sweet lady there and she said, "Sir, I think you are correct." She then gave me a lot of paperwork on the things I would need to do in order to make this dream a reality. So I started right there. I didn't even let my family know this time because I didn't want to get their hopes up again until I was sure I could make it happen.

I started working on this huge checklist to start this Hot Dog Cart business. About 6 months into this I decided it was too much for me to accomplish everything on this checklist. I said forget it I quit, they were right, it's too hard to start a Hot Dog Stand business here. As soon as I said that, I got in my car and there was a song playing on the radio, Mary, Mary (Go Get Your Blessing). Just like that, I picked the fight for my dreams right back up!

It took me 6 more months to finish the checklist and get approved by the Health Department. I was so happy to take my completed checklist back to them to start this process. I was then informed by the lady up front I would have to take all this paperwork to the manager over the business licenses for him to sign off on it. That's right, the same guy that told me it would never happen. At that very instance, I felt like all of that hard work I just did was in vain, that guy had already told me it would never happen.

I walked on in the back to get it signed and they informed me that the guy was on vacation, and his assistant would have to sign off on it! Just like that, I had finally started the first-ever Hot Dog Stand in downtown Montgomery. I couldn't wait to go home and tell my family! So I gathered my family right back together and told them we were about to start the Hot Dog business called That's My DOG! A place where you can have a hot dog any way you want it, pork, beef, turkey, chicken, or veggie. They were like man; you know the city is not about to let that happen. That's when I whipped out my Business License like, BAM!

As soon as the manager from the business licenses department came back from his vacation he gave me a call. He said, "I see you were able to sneak through while I was out, you better be lucky I was on vacation because I would have sent you packing just like the rest of them." I said, "Well sir, I hope you had the best vacation EVER!"

About two days later I had the pleasure of meeting him as he so rudely came to the cart telling me what I can and can't do on the cart. I would see him about twice a week, all negative experiences. It was like he was trying to get me to quit. When he wasn't coming to yell at me very rudely, I could see him sitting in his car just watching me. About twice a week he would come out yelling, "BOY, didn't I tell you that you couldn't have this, or "BOY, you can't do that." To the point I felt like he was harassing me. I said to myself, I can't make a living this way, what I should do is to sue the entire city on his behalf, this was definitely harassment. Before I could do that, I had to go and read everything they had about outdoor vending in the city of Montgomery.

As I started reading, I started discovering a lot of stuff he was telling me I couldn't do was nowhere to be found in the downtown vending ordinance. So the next time he came down, he jumped out of the car yelling, "BOY, didn't I tell you that you couldn't have them chairs out here." I said, "Sir, I just want to make sure we are on the same page. If you look here on the ordinance code 5, section 6, it says I can't have anything for sale that is not attached to the cart, well sir, I'm not trying to sale my chairs, I'm just trying to have somewhere to sit." He looked at it and then said, "Well, you can keep them", then he left.

About a week later, they began construction on Dexter AVE and I had to go around the corner on Lawrence St. He came right on out there yelling, "BOY, you know you can't be on this street, pack this stuff up and get off this street ASAP." I packed it all up and went to go get my map of where the ordinance covered. After I was able to find the map, I brought it to his office. He looked at me and said, "What do you need now, Mr. Lee?" As if I was the one that had been coming to harass him (LoL). I said, "Sir, I just want to make sure we are on the same page." He said, "Nope, you know you can't be on that street." I gave him the paper and he looked at it and said, "Ok, you can go back out there." Not once did I get an apology.

So the clubs were picking up around the Alley in downtown Montgomery. With the majority of the people coming out around 10 pm. However, it was in the ordinance for me to be off the streets by 10 pm. I went down to 25th and Washington to the Zoning department and I asked them what could I do to stay out later to serve the people coming out of the clubs. They said, "Well Mr. Lee, the only way you can do that is to rewrite the entire downtown vending ordinance." I asked, "Can I do that?" They said, "Yes sir, it's a process that you will need to go through, but you can do it." So that was my new mission!

After I rewrote the downtown vending ordinance, I had to first get it signed by the Zoning department. I then had to go through the county to have them sign off on it. The the last place was the Montgomery City Council and the Mayor. I stood there before them pleading my case as to why I should stay out past 10 pm. My case was this, all of the bars stayed open until at least 2 pm and all the other food sources closed by 11 pm. I asked them, "Do we want people to come out of our downtown bars drinking all night and not have an opportunity to get something to eat before getting into their cars causing them to possibly get a DUI? Allow me to give them a hotdog to sober up a little before driving home."

Everyone seemed to think it was a great idea. Then all of a sudden the Mayor called up the manager over the Business Licenses, I thought to myself where did he come from (LoL). They asked him, "Sir, what do you think about this idea?" He said, "All I can say is, Mr. Lee knows all of the rules in the ordinance and thus far he follows everyone one of them, so I see no problem with it." Just like that my version of the New downtown ordinance was approved.

So now when you go downtown to 25th and Washington, you can see the downtown vending ordinance wrote by yours truly, the "Boy with NO NAME" - Charles Lee. That's a Little small piece of Black History in Montgomery, Alabama (LoL).

Now that business was booming with That's My Dog, my Mentoring Program had slowed down. God spoke to me again and said, "Now that I gave you this business and it's doing well, it's now time for you to go back to doing my mission." That mission was mentoring the youth, so I gave it another shot.

Since everyone knew me from That's My Dog, we decided to call our mentoring program, "That's My Child." Just like we were taking ownership of the hot dogs, we wanted to take ownership of the youth because a lot of times you see a young person going through a hard time, such as their pants falling off their waist, or they are always on the corner looking like trouble, you just pass them right by shaking your head in disgust. You know why? That's NOT your child! However, what if it WAS your child? Wouldn't you want someone to stop, pull over and offer your child that same Love, Compassion, and Support?

We wanted to send this as a reminder that the next time you see a child in need, stop and Love on him/her just as if that was your child. It could very well be yours tomorrow, if you were to leave this earth!

Chapter 23

Charles Lee Jr

Two things my mother told me the doctor told her about my birth.

1. *My chances of surviving to the age of five years old were slim to none.*

2. *If I survived, I would never be able to have kids.*

I always looked at myself as a father figure to most of my nephews, niece's, and little cousins. Especially those whose fathers weren't in their life, but I was still not their father.

All I ever wanted to be was a great father! At one point we decided that we would try to have kids but it didn't work so we just kind of gave up. Then about 5 years later we were decided to try to have a kid again. So, we reached out to a friend who had about 7 kids already and was pregnant with the 8th. We said to ourselves, "If anyone knows the secret to getting pregnant, it would be her!"

We reached out to her to ask her the secret. She said at first that she didn't know but after her third child, she was pretty sure of what was happening. She said every time that she would get pregnant, it would be right after her cycle. So, after Mohona's next cycle, that day after, I gave it everything I had and left it in the Lords' hands (LoL).

About 7 weeks later I was walking in the door on report card day at about 8 pm, tired from working all-day. Laurali greeted me saying, "Hello dad how are you?" She said, "Let me warm up your food for you while you sit down and relax. I was thinking to myself why is she being so nice today, what is today? Then I remembered, it was report card day. I said to her, "You're trying to distract me, where is your report card?"

She said, "Dad, that's not all that important right now", I said, "Oh no?" She said, "There's something that's way more important that I need to talk to you about." I replied, "Oh yeah, what can be more important than us talking about this report card?" She said, "I want to tell you but I'm not supposed to tell you, I think I might get a whooping if I tell you." I said, "Now you definitely have to tell me, I have to know what you're talking about." Still persistent about not telling me she said, "If I tell you, you have to promise that you won't tell mama I told you or I will have to run away because mama told me if I told you I was going to get a whooping."

There was a pregnancy test box on the table that she slapped down to the floor, but I wasn't paying attention to the box. Then she said, "Pay attention to the box." Then I started to think to myself, this is a distraction; she's just trying to get my mind off her report card so I said to her, "Girl, go get me the report card right now." She said, "Dad, you're still not getting it! Okay, the last clue!" Then she put clothes under a shirt to make it as if her belly was swollen and she said, "What happens when a person looks like this?" I was like "Are you trying to tell me you're pregnant?" She said, "Not me, but someone in this house is." So I said, "Mama pregnant?" She started shaking her head up and down while jogging in place. I said, "Stop playing!" She said, "Mama took three pregnancy tests and all three of them said positive". We started searching every trash can in the house for the pregnancy test but couldn't find any of them. That night we laid on the couch, Laurali and I, until 2 am thinking of names for girls and boys. This was one of the sweetest days of my life.

A couple of months later we found out it was a boy and we decide to name him Charles Anthony Bryson Lee Jr. She wanted his name to have Anthony in it like her dad. Then Bryson because we had a friend that was pregnant around the same time that we were pregnant and she miscarried. She had planned to name him Bryson. So we gave him the name Bryson in remembrance of her son. They were pleased with his name being Bryson. Charles Anthony Bryson Lee Jr., aka, CJ.

He was born on October 3rd, 2016, at 5 am. She was so ready for the baby to come out, she called while I was working and said she was on her way to the hospital. When I arrived at the hospital they couldn't find a heartbeat for CJ so they admitted her. We were there for about two days when they let us know that if he didn't come out soon they would have to break her water. On the third day, we thought they might have to go ahead and do an emergency C-section. However, on the third day at 5 am the little booger was ready to see the world and out he came headfirst! They had to cut mama to get his big head out and I was trying to watch the whole process but my stomach couldn't handle it. I still have nightmares till this Day (LoL). It was worth every minute though. We were so happy to meet that little fella.

Chapter 24

That's

My

child

So, here I was running a successful Hot Dog Cart business, just opened up a store front on West Jeff Davis located in the West/downtown-ish area of Montgomery, thanks to some awesome Pastors at Light of the World Ministries Church which was next door. I was serving my purpose every evening with an after-school program called That's My Child at the Chisholm Community Center where our mission was to mentor the youth through arts and education.

We did a poll of all of the kids that were coming into the center and asked them exactly what they wanted to see in the Community Center. They let us know they would like to see dance, poetry, theater, sign language, and modeling. We reached out to different colleges such as, Alabama State University, Huntingdon College, and Auburn of Montgomery (AUM), to see if we could get young professionals to come out and help us with the programs and it worked.

We offered free arts with only one requirement, if you participate in the arts, you had to participate in tutoring beforehand. That was the education component. Slowly it begin to grow, the more we took the art kids out to different venues to perform, a lot of the other kids from the community wanted to evolve. Before we knew it, we were hosting about 70 to 80 kids in this one area at Chisholm Community Center. Sometimes the senior citizens would need that room on some evenings which would leave us with nowhere to practice.

We started looking for space, the journey had begun. I noticed across the street from That's My Dog physical location, there was a building for sale. I inquired about the building and was told that it would be $50,000 to purchase. Even though the building was pretty small I knew we needed the space so I began trying to raise funds to purchase the building. We did fundraisers and all kinds of campaigns, I even personally prayed and fasted for this building. We raised about $387 in about 6 months.

On that 7th month, we saw the for-sale sign had been taken down and people began to move in there. I can remember going to speak with Pastor Huffman that day and I asked him, "Why didn't God bless me with that building." He told me that he believed that building was way too small for what God wanted to do with my ministry, He just believed God had greater for me.

Shortly thereafter, about 3 months later, a nice gentleman heard about what we were doing through a mutual friend and he let me know he had a space with 10,000 square feet and would love for us to come to use the building for the ministry. We considered it because he was willing to give us 20 years free but, the work that was needing to be done to the building would cost more than we could afford. Even worse, it was outside of the area we were already serving which was North Montgomery. This building was located in West Montgomery. In which, there was another Ministry that was also located in West Montgomery called Common Ground, helping inner-city youth as well.

One day I was talking to the director there, I was telling him the struggles I was facing about getting this building located in West Montgomery and he informed me that it was a building in North Montgomery in my area that was about to go up for sale. I reached out to the ministry that was looking to sell in North Montgomery and scheduled a tour to come by and check out the campus. My board, chairman, and I went to check out the campus. Not only was there one amazing building, but there were four different amazing buildings on a gated campus with vans and school buses to sell all for such an awesome price.

We offered them full asking price, and they left every single thing that we needed to start our nonprofit the right way. Very nice office desk, chairs, phone system already connected, filing cabinets, everything you would need to run a ministry, all we needed to do was sweep up, and they even left brooms (LoL).

On November 30th, 2017 we purchased the location for our ministry. At this point we had seven different programs going on, still coaching basketball, still doing after school art programs, and still were doing after school tutoring. We also started a Barbershop book club, getting 13 Barbershops to agree to us putting bookshelves in their Barbershop for young kids to read and trade their book report out for a free haircut.

In 2015 we launched a program inside of the alternative school systems in Montgomery to take young men through a 9-week curriculum. The individual Mentor, Tutor, and Counselor worked to change the behaviors and give them the motivation to become leaders called, Gents-2-Gentlemen, which was near and dear to my heart.

As we were coming up with different names to name the campus, God showed me the vision coming to pass, The Spot! I said we will call it, THE SPOT! Our program director at the time said oh yeah, like

S.P.O.T: Students Pouring Out Talent. It was a perfect fit because of the vision of The S.P.O.T. in the beginning and this was everything in those dreams plus more.

We welcomed our students to the new facility and they loved it. There were four buildings, one building was set up for learning, the second building was set up as a place to give out free groceries to the community, the third space was set up as a thrift store, and the fourth building was the main building, it was set up as a church and it had a commercial kitchen inside.

We did an assessment of all of our older students, new students and students in the community asking them what they would like to see in these spaces in the community. During the assessments, there were three common answers:

1. The Students still wanted the Arts.

2. Lots of students wanted to find jobs and work.

3. A lot of students wanted to own their own business.

We decided to increase the mission. Our new mission would be to mentor the youth through Arts, Education, Entrepreneurship and Workforce Development. We slowly begin to paint each building the color it represented with yellow being the building for Education, purple being the building for the Arts, green being the building for Entrepreneurship, and the red being the building for Workforce Development.

Although all of the programs were going pretty well, the best we could do with only a staff of three, with over one hundred students, we decided to focus on what most of our students wanted and at that particular time, it was jobs. They said they had been going to fill out job applications, but no one would give them a chance. I was thinking, well you do know that you can't go to a job interview with flip flops on or your pants sagging or earbuds in your ears or 20 minutes late with a great excuse. I started to realize more and more that maybe they didn't realize this.

We then decided to start a Teens To Work program, students 14 to 19, that focused on job readiness skills that would get them ready for their first job in the Workforce Development. We started graduating lots of students and creating partnerships with lots of jobs that we're looking to hire high school students. However, a lot of our students still were not getting hired after graduating from the program. So since God blessed me with the wisdom to be able to open up a restaurant I decided we would open up a restaurant for them so they would be able to have a place to work.

Chapter 25

What the Devil

Meant for Evil

We moved into That's My Child's new facility known as The S.P.O.T! Looking around I had both of my sisters there mentoring and helping in so many ways. My oldest sister, Latasha, was the dance coach and she also started a mentoring program with the young ladies at TMC called Young & Classy. This program was a great way to build relationships with the young ladies in the community, to build a sisterhood with life-long goals for their future. Reminding them not to get pregnant before marriage because their lives had value and also to always remain classy! This was perfect for my oldest sister, because not only did she get pregnant at such a young age, she had three girls!

Since day one, she was a great mother. I mean solid! To this day I never figured out how she was so strong. She raised three beautiful girls, and she made sure they were as strong as she was. She would always tell them; I made these mistakes so you all don't have to. I also remember asking her one day when she was about 18 years old what she wanted to do. She told me that she wanted to help young ladies!

My middle sister, Angela was the Driver, Cook, Personal Assistant, and everything we asked her to do. She connected with the guys in the Gents-2-Gentlemen program. I strongly believe it was because not only did she become pregnant with a young man at the age of 13, she gave birth to 3 young men, which gave her the advantage of knowing how young men thought. She also had a beautiful daughter as well; I was always super surprised by her strength.

I remember being in Jr. High with her, everyone just couldn't believe she was pregnant and would have so much to say. She never walked with her head down, and I respected her so much for that. I still remember both of my sisters telling me within months of each other that they were pregnant. I had two thoughts that ran through my mind;

1. Did I not do a good job of protecting them as a brother?

2. How are they going to finish school as new parents?

All I knew was that I was committed from that day forward, whatever they needed, I wanted to make sure I could help. I was there for both of their child births. I stayed there throughout the whole labor up until it was time to cut the umbilical cord.

My mother is also heavily involved in the organization. She comes to The S.P.O.T every evening and every child there calls her Grandma Lee. She has dedicated her life to making sure that she provides love to every child there. She truly goes above and beyond the call of duty to make sure every child on this campus has what they need. I know she has some regrets as to how we were raised, and there's nothing she can do to change that, so she makes up for it now, by bettering every young person's life she comes in contact with! I love seeing how loving, nurturing, and supportive she is with the students at TMC. It truly makes my heart smile.

As far as my dad goes, Lord knows we have had our ups and downs. I think throughout the years of seeing him battle with this addiction and being in and out of jail, it taught me one thing, how to appreciate life one day at a time! For the past year since my dad has been released from his last prison sentence, he has been sober! Not only has he been sober, but he has been helping out BIG TIME! He has been helping out by running the busiest cart we have with That's My Dog. Helping to train with new employees, as well as keeping me motivated. Not only that, he has he been able to make money to help support his family.

Every Thursday he hosts a Bible Study for our family, so as we do the work to empower our Community, he keeps us lifted in prayer and comes to The Spot all the time to help with maintenance. The devil thought he would destroy my family while we were very young and immature, instead, God took everything that we went through and dipped it in his blood so he could use it for his glory. Now we use it every day to empower families in our community because we know exactly what it's like to be a broken family. That is our number one tool, to help families in our Community.

Chapter 26

That's

My

Dog Jr.

My family was all together doing what we know best, plus, God had blessed me with some of the best staff members, and volunteers I could have ever prayed for. We witness students go from failing classes to making A&B honor roll, to students that were dropping out of school, to graduating high school. Students that were going to the Juvenile Detention Facility, to signing up and joining the military. Students that were selling drugs, are now becoming young Entrepreneurs. Students that were breaking into houses in the neighborhood, are now students that are getting jobs. Don't get me wrong, we were seeing great growth within the community, but we were still losing great students as well.

From watching students drop out of school, to visiting students in the hospital from gunshot wounds. To burying students that didn't survive and visiting students in jail, watching young girls drop out of the program because of pregnancy. We never decided to focus on the students we lost, no more than what we could've done better. Instead, we focused on saving one child at a time! We always say, if we can just change one child, then our work here at TMC is not in vain.

The more students were hearing about That's My Child being the place to get them jobs, the more students were coming to The S.P.O.T. At one point we were graduating more students then we could find jobs for. So, with more and more students coming by looking for jobs, we tried to partner with more business in the community. Restaurants, skating rinks, even the local Go-karting place in Montgomery called, Go Karting Montgomery. We decided to partner with them because they believed in a better future for our youth and they wanted to allow students to work.

However, we still couldn't keep up with the number of students coming in looking to work. At this time I started to feel overwhelmed with running That's My Dog, That's My Child, being a father, a husband, my commitment at the church as the Youth Pastor, and as a Community Leader. I just didn't know how to balance it all so I started to pray and ask God why I was feeling so overwhelmed. He said, "I didn't give you That's My Dog to become a millionaire, I gave it to you as a tool for my ministry." As I reflected on all of the accomplishments I was awarded, the great relationship with the Mayor, Chief of Police, Sheriff, and so many other businesses, and professional people, I was reminded that it had all come from me being a well-respected businessman in the community.

All of a sudden a huge green light went off! I can remember thinking, since I am having a hard time finding job placement for our students, why don't I do the same thing I did when it was hard for me to find a job, just create one for them. God was reminding me of that restaurant at The S.P.O.T that I use to see in the vision. Only this time I had all the tools/ knowledge I needed to start a restaurant.

I gathered all of the students together and told them we were about to start the first ever all managed and operated teenage restaurant in the country called, That's My Dog Jr. They were all so excited just to know that they would be earning a paycheck. I was also excited thinking about how much we can develop a student in the workplace, not only could we help with math with the cash flow, but we could also do conflict resolution with customer service. We could also deal with boosting confidence, and self-esteem as well as so many other factors in Youth Development.

As scary as it was, we were able to pull it off with That's My Dog Jr becoming a major attraction in the city. Celebrities would come to visit such as rapper, Lil Boosie, NFL # 3 draft pick, Quinnen Williams and so many others. Nothing made me happier in my whole career in mentoring than to see the faces on the students as they received their first paycheck. Priceless!

The first time most of them seen their hard work pay off. The second time was when a group of Senators gave them the proclamation for starting the first-ever teenage restaurant in Montgomery, Alabama. They were awarded this Proclamation at the State House where lots of Civil Rights leaders had to come to challenge laws and make history. For the first time they as teenagers were creating history for themselves. Such a monumental moment!

That day I went home, and for some reason, my Birth Certificate was on the nightstand staring at me, still with no name. I could hear God's voice so clearly saying, "Always remember I am GOD, and I can take anyone's test in life and turn it into a Testimony." Then my wife came into the room and said, "Baby guest what?" I said, "What!" She said, "God has blessed us again, I'm pregnant!"

Testimonial

Being able to be the first Marketing Manager at That's My Dog Jr. is a blessing. Don't get me wrong though, it has been very challenging. I came into a military family at the age of seven. You can say I was always somewhat of a rebel. I've always been smart in school but for some reason I was always getting into trouble, getting into fights. My family was so concerned about my behavior that I was sent to a military school for two years to work on my attitude and learn some discipline.

I was very tall and big for my age, so my family was afraid that one more fight might land me in serious trouble where I might be kicked out of school for good. I believe my attitude change came from me being able to appreciate and embrace the opportunity given to me by That's My Dog, Jr.

It was truly a divine intervention on how my life began. My mom Louise, had been going through a rough time and she went to church seeking a little help. My grandmother Jackie, was the church secretary at the time. My grandmother told me that after talking to my mom, she could tell that she was someone special. It wasn't long before my mom and grandmother developed a bond that would only deepen over time this allowed my mom to become very close to my aunts.

Although my mom worked very hard, we still didn't have a lot of money. When I was seven, my mom fell ill and passed away. I had always been close to my family but it became legal after my mom passed and my grandmother became my legal guardian. Both of my aunts loved me very much. My aunt, which lived in Montgomery, promised my mom that she would continue to look after me and help my grandmother raise me, I consider her my other mom.

Eventually, my auntie signed me up for the Teens To Work Program. The program taught me so much about the workforce. For instance, I used to think that getting a job was just filling out an application and they tell you yes or no. It turned out there was a whole process to go through if you wanted to secure a job.

The program takes three weeks to complete. In the first week, we went over soft skills and how important they are. That week taught me the importance of body language, a firm handshake, etc. The second week was about how to fill out an application, how to properly dress for an interview, and how to conduct yourself in the interview. The third week taught us how to move up in the company to the position of a manager.

After I completed the course I filled out an application for multiple jobs, Mr. Charles was the only person that gave me a chance. He gave me the position of Marketing Manager. Besides knowing how to get followers, because every 15-year-old kid wants to be Instafamous, there was a learning curve and Mr. Charles was with me every step of the way. He took time out of his schedule to put me in contact with different mentors. I had to learn how to open up to people so that I could resonate with them.

It was weird going to Wal-Mart and people stop and ask if you're the person they saw on tv. I had to learn how to present myself in a professional way which has helped me more times than I can count. I had to learn the ins and outs of Facebook and Instagram. Becoming familiar with the analytics was very confusing but with the help of YouTube, I was able to learn the ins and outs.

As a Marketing Manager, I also needed to be able to come up with different promotions and ad campaigns. I learned how to network and build a relationship with our previous Mayor, Todd Strange. I got the opportunity to meet Congressmen and be able to be a part of a state resolution, declaring that we are the first teens to run a restaurant in the state of Alabama.

It was truly a blessing to be at the Statehouse, the same place where Martin Luther King Jr stood so naturally, I made sure that I took a selfie.

Anthony Drake

Made in the USA
Columbia, SC
10 December 2019